DR. GEORGE
WASHINGTON CARVER
Scientist

George Washington Carver started his life as
a sickly, orphaned Negro slave baby, but his
thirst for knowledge and his determination
to become a scientist made him one of the
most honored men of his time. He experi-
mented with peanuts and sweet potatoes, getting hundreds of new products from both.
He utilized waste materials and made roads
out of cotton, insulating boards out of corn
stalks, paper from wisteria, pottery out of red
clay. He refused staggering salaries to work
elsewhere, and remained at his small laboratory at Tuskegee College until his death.

DR. GEORGE WASHINGTON CARVER

DR. GEORGE
WASHINGTON CARVER
Scientist

BY SHIRLEY GRAHAM AND
GEORGE D. LIPSCOMB

ILLUSTRATED BY ELTON C. FAX

JULIAN MESSNER

New York

Copyright 1944 by Simon & Schuster, Inc.

© *renewed 1971 by Shirley Graham and George D. Lipscomb*

Thirty-first Printing, 1979

ISBN 0-671-32510-8

PRINTED IN THE UNITED STATES OF AMERICA

Telegrams sent to Tuskegee Institute

The White House
Washington, D. C.
January 6, 1943

The world of science has lost one of its most eminent figures and the race from which he sprang an outstanding member in the passing of Dr. George Washington Carver. The versatility of his genius and his achievements in diverse branches of the arts and sciences were truly amazing. All mankind are the beneficiaries of his discoveries in the field of agricultural chemistry. The things which he achieved in the face of early handicaps will for all time afford an inspiring example to youth everywhere. I count it a great privilege to have met Dr. Carver and to have talked with him at Tuskegee on the happy occasion of my visit to the Institute which was the scene of his long and distinguished labors.

(Signed) FRANKLIN D. ROOSEVELT.

Washington, D. C.
January 7, 1943

When Dr. Carver died the United States lost one of its finest Christian gentlemen. He was a good friend of my father and mother and I had known him for forty-seven years. To the world he was known as a scientist. Those who knew him best, however, realize that his outstanding characteristic was a strong feeling of the eminence of God. Everything he was and did found its origin in that strong and continuous feeling.

(Signed) H. A. WALLACE,
Vice-President of the United States.

A letter from Mr. O. D. Foster, lecturer, writer, member of Inter-American Affairs Committee, and a friend of Dr. Carver.

COSMOS CLUB
Washington, D. C.

January 15, 1943

Dear Miss Graham:

From the bottom of my heart, you have my most sincere longings for your success while you affectionately labor on one of the most difficult of assignments, and yet on one of the greatest of privileges—mediating to a world so incapable of understanding and of appreciating the mysteriously unique George Washington Carver. May you take courage in the knowledge that if you fully encompassed for us his greatness in all its breadth and richness, we would need another mediator to interpret you.

Although it took the Almighty geological ages, through His natural creative process, to crush humble black coal into precious sparkling diamonds, through the delicate fingers of Dr. Carver, He all but instantly transformed common everyday objects into a thousand products of millions of evaluations.

With but a few discarded objects salvaged from backyards and dump heaps for his most humble laboratory, his fertile mind gave to the world over a half a hundred creations, any one of which would have honored the most elaborately equipped laboratory of our greatest universities.

Who ever shattered bonds more binding, attained freedom more divinely and served mankind more universally? To whom else can the student look for a comparable example? To what more brilliant and more enticing star can he hitch his wagon? Of such another, history has honored us with no record.

To me Dr. Carver was one of the very few truly great characters of all time.

Humbly yours,
(Signed) O. D. FOSTER.

CONTENTS

PART III—AND THE FULLNESS, THEREOF

PART I

I WILL LIFT UP MINE EYES

"From the life of men whose passage is marked by a trace of durable light, let us piously gather up every word, every incident likely to make known the incentives of their great soul, for the education of posterity."

LOUIS PASTEUR.

1. WASHINGTON—1921

Two MORNING TRAINS rolled panting under the long sheds of the Union Station and discharged their passengers—one train from New York City, the other from the deep South. Red Caps scurried about and wheeled trucks piled high with luggage. Now, against the great barrel vaults of the huge waiting room, echoed the sound of many feet. Light filtering through the high-placed windows fell upon the hurrying, impatient travelers from all parts of the country. Indeed, they come from all parts of the world, and, passing out into the pillared portico pause a moment on this impressive threshold of Washington, capital of the United States.

Just within the door, jostled to one side by the crowd, the tall, slightly stooped black man staggered as someone pushed against the large wooden case he carried by its iron handle. Stopping, he let it rest gently on the floor, then pulling the old golf cap from his head, passed his hand over his close-cropped, graying hair. He lifted his head and looked out over the crowd. A weather-tanned traveler, hurrying from the dim recesses of the waiting room towards the train gates glanced up and then turned, sharply staring. By Jove, it was time he came home! Certainly, he had been too long digging among Egyptian ruins. For there, before the startled eyes of the archaeologist, silhouetted in the doorway appeared to be the head of a Pharaoh. Of course, it couldn't be, but there it was—the finely shaped skull, sweeping forehead, the high, proud nose, delicate nostrils flaring at base, sharp cheekbones and thin lips. As if aware of the searching gaze, the man turned and looked at him. The traveler blinked! It was the face of a Negro, a poor, working-class Negro. But, for a moment—he turned away quickly. That night, just before he went to sleep, the famous archaeologist thought about it again. He could still see those eyes, set so wide apart, and burning with a strange intensity.

The dark man, unaware of all this speculation, shrank back further from the crowd, nervously replaced his cap and drew his overcoat closer about his thin frame as if to seek protection in its threadbare folds. His eyes brightened as he saw a Red Cap hurrying in his direction. But the porter, head up as if looking for someone, and peering around the crowd of people did not see him until the quivering voice brought him to a halt.

"Ah—ah—could you help me with this—case?"

Quickly the Red Cap took in the pathetic figure, noting the ill-fitting, shapeless trousers, the broken shoes with bits of mud worn into the creases.

His voice was kind as he said, "Sorry, Pops, I'd like to, but I been sent down to meet a ve-ry *important* man—a big scientist come all the way from *Tuskegee* and I daren't miss him."

"I—I—," the high voice began—but the Red Cap was already bobbing away in the crowd. Across the man's face flickered an amused grin. The little mustache wiggled a moment. He chuckled.

"Now, I hope that nice man won't lose too much time looking for that—big scientist!" he murmured the words softly, then chuckled again.

His nervousness had vanished and, picking up the case, he moved quickly across the stone floor. It was a rather queer, unusual gait—that of a man braced against strong outdoor winds, leaning slightly forward, his feet slipping a little as if unused to hard smooth floors. Yet he moved lightly and easily through the crowd and came out the great central doors. In the early morning sunshine lay Washington. Without a glance up the long, cloister-like corridors, he stepped from the curb and started across the runways. A taxi ground its brakes and a policeman yelled, "Look out there, old man!"

Unheeding, he hurried across the street car tracks, his eyes fixed on the lifting monument with its green plot, and on the opening vista of lovely, wide avenues.

Spring had come early that year to Washington. It was 1921—one of the gala years so soon after our first great Armistice Day. People were still rejoicing that all wars were over! Patches of snow lay about in crevices, but the green of tiny blades showed through the mud. As he climbed the little stairs of the circle's podium, the black man seemed to grow. His loosened overcoat flapped in the breeze. Pulling off his cap, he threw back his head, breathing deeply as if stretching cramped lungs. It was good to be outdoors again, under God's blue sky!

At this moment, a colored taxi-driver on the other side of the circle saw him. He called, "Taxi, sir?"

But as his fare approached, the taxi-driver's face fell and he turned away.

"Yes," the high, thin voice was saying, "I'd like a taxi." He waited patiently.

The driver eyed him suspiciously. "Where you going?"

The man's eyes swept the scene before him, pausing a moment on the white dome of the Capitol.

"I'm going—to the—," he hesitated, drawing from his pocket a large old-fashioned watch. "I've lots of time— and for me," he regarded the driver quizzically, "that is very unusual. Time must not be wasted." He looked about him. "This is a beautiful city. And we have the same name—this city and I. I'd like to see it. Could you drive me around?"

Instead of answering the question, the driver asked one. "Your name Washington?"

"My name is George Washington Carver," answered the man simply.

"That's a mighty high-soundin' name," commented the driver, his eyes on the broken shoes. "Well," he heaved himself into his seat, "sight-seeing trips are three dollars a hour!"

He was frankly surprised when George Washington Carver climbed into the back seat, after carefully lifting in the heavy wooden case.

"Want I should take it up here?" obliged the driver, indicating the case.

"Oh, no!" the answer came very quickly, then, as if apologizing for the vehemence, "I'll take care of it, thank you."

"Where you want to go?" The driver did not sound interested.

"I'd like to see the big trees growing around the White House, and some of those fine, old trees lining the avenues, and oh, yes—the delicate, young cherry trees they've sent all the way from Japan. I—"

The driver's mouth had fallen open. "Trees? Is that all you want to see—trees?"

"Well, no," his passenger smiled. "There's lots of fine shrubbery too, and—the Zoological Park. We mustn't miss that!"

"Humph!" grunted the taxi-driver. He shrugged his shoulders, dismissing all responsibility and pressed heavily on the gas.

Back in the Union Station, two officials of the United Peanut Growers Association paced the waiting room anxiously.

"That's why I took this early train from New York," said one. "I was sure I'd catch him when he got here. It's essential we tell him what to say. What would he know about tariff?"

"Do you suppose he hasn't come?" The second man was watching the doorway.

"If he hasn't, we might as well give up. We'll never get a look-in on that Hawley-Smoot bill without him. There are some colored people over there. Do you suppose—?" the first man examined the group intently.

"How would *I* know him?" the question was impatient. "Here's the porter now. Maybe he—"

"Boss," the porter was panting, "I sure ain't see him nowhere. I watched every living soul got off that there Dixie Flyer."

"Guess we've missed him." The first man turned away, after handing the porter a half dollar.

The porter grinned. "Thank *you!* Can I get you-all a taxi?"

"Might as well, Bill." The second man tried to sound optimistic. "Maybe he came up last night. Anyhow, we're not due at the Senate until two o'clock. Come on, let's go to the hotel. I haven't had breakfast."

"Neither have I. My head's splitting. Never can sleep in those confounded berths." The taxi had come to a stop at the curb. They climbed in.

"Where to, sir?" the driver's voice is respectful.

"The Mayflower," answered the big man. He relaxed in his seat. "He promised, Bill, and from what I've heard about George Washington Carver, he'll keep his word."

The taxi whirled around the circle, narrowly missing a rather ramshackle cab driven by a colored driver who, still pondering over his peculiar passenger, did not see them coming.

Two hours later this same driver was peacefully rolling down Connecticut Avenue at what can best be described as a holiday pace. The old man had said "go slow" and Pete was going slow. For, by now, Pete was thoroughly convinced that his fare was *somebody in particular*. He'd have something really interesting to tell the boys that night.

It had happened at the Zoological Park which they had just left. Nobody had even looked up when they went in. Yes, he'd followed the old man. His talk about trees was like nothing he had ever heard. He'd never known before trees were just like people and needed to be "loved." Well, they were walking down a little lane, when suddenly the old man had stopped, and let out a little yell. He got right down on his hands and knees and crawled under a wire and there he was sort of huddled up over a bunch of leaves, saying queer things in a breathless sort of way. One of the attendants came running. He stood staring till the old man looked up and snapped something at him. Why, he'd seemed to scare that attendant out of his wits. Soon a half dozen men were right down there on the ground. And the old man had started showing them something about the plant. He'd lift one leaf after another and rub his long finger along the back.

Everybody listened and then they got a spade and took the leafy bunch right out of the ground, the old man telling them every minute to be careful. They carried it into the greenhouse and by that time a white-haired very important gentleman had come. He shook the old man's hand like he was tickled to death to see him.

And right out loud Pete heard him say, "You're the greatest"—now, what was the word—yes, *my-col-o-gist* in the country!"

Doggone! What a swell word! Pete kept saying it over and over again—"my-col-o-gist." He wanted to remember it. Not that he had the slightest idea what it meant, but

Pete was certain that any time white folks call a colored man anything sounded like *that*—the colored man sure was *somebody*. And they'd told him to come back again and then they gave him lots of little green leaves that he put inside that big old wooden box, and when he left they said, "Good-bye, Doctor Carver!"

Pete glanced into the little mirror above his head. Dr. Carver had taken off his overcoat and now in the lapel of his almost green alpaca jacket was stuck a small fresh flower. He sat with his arms folded, head falling forward. Pete slowed up a little.

"Let him sleep," he thought, "I'll bet he's dog tired."

He was tired. The trip from Tuskegee had been long. Colored people could not ride in Pullman cars in the south, even when they had the money, and he had been forced to sit up all night in a smoky, close car. The sight of the poisonous fungus hidden beneath the delicate leaves of that rare plant had unnerved him. How could the gardeners be so careless! Yet, they wouldn't have known. He had identified it immediately as a disease from the jungles of India—and here it was cropping up in a park in Washington. He shuddered to think of the havoc which might have been wrought.

His hand went out and touched the precious case now bearing the leaves which would be the subject of his next paper to the Department of Agriculture. He could hardly wait to get back to his laboratory. He sighed deeply. He still had that speech he'd promised to make—couldn't go back until that was done. What if he had not gone to the Gardens? But, then, of course, he had been directed. He never would have set out on this trip to Washington in the first place had God not directed him to do so. He hadn't known about the sick plant. But God knew.

Now he must go before that Senate Committee. Imagine him being called to speak right inside the Capitol itself! What was he going to say? Well, he'd just leave that to God, too. He wouldn't worry.

How far He had brought him!

Did they know? Could they see him now—riding through the streets of Washington—would they hear his speech—big, red Farmer Carver and his wife—Frau Carver? So long ago and yet there they were looming up behind the first memories of his childhood. The big, Lutheran Bible, much too heavy for him to lift, but at night the slow, thick voice of the farmer reading "I will lift up mine eyes to the hills—I will lift up mine eyes—" Today they seemed very near.

He leaned back and closed his eyes. For him, the great, white marble buildings of Washington vanished and in their place there rose the Ozark hills and all the people and the things of long ago were real again.

2. WAS THE TINY BOY WORTH A HORSE?

"*Heraus! Heraus mit sie!* I say—get up!"

It was still dark outside, but down in the kitchen the German farmer was shaking the wooden ladder that led to the boy's place under the eaves.

"Get up—you! *Raus mit!* Or—must I come up?" Now the voice was threatening and the tiny black boy shivered as he tumbled off his pallet. They said he was six or seven years old, plenty old enough to milk the cow, tend the hog and chickens and do something about keeping weeds from choking the already sparse garden. But the rusty little legs and arms were like pipe-stems, his hands bony, with long, curling fingers, his face was pinched. In that little dark face, his eyes burned like coals of fire. And, even though he could not speak, Frau Carver had noted that he saw everything.

Yesterday, he had hoed in the garden for many hours. His back still ached with fatigue. Now, spindly legs still trembling with sleep, he clumsily crawled down the ladder and there in the kitchen was Frau Carver, still swathed in yards and yards of sleeping clothes, on her head a nightcap. But how glad he was to see her!

"No! No, *mein Mann*," she was saying to her husband. "He is too small. After yesterday, he is too tired. I have work for him to do in the house this morning. He cannot go."

"And who will help me in the fields?" the farmer asked angrily. "Have we money? Our crops, poor as they are, will rot. We will starve and he also!"

"God is good," the woman's voice was soothing. "Not a sparrow falls that he does not know. Let be the little fellow. Soon he will be big and strong." The little boy's eyes were fast upon her, drinking in every word.

"*O weh!*" exploded Farmer Carver. "I had a *horse—*" he paused significantly, "and now," his eyes fell on the shrinking little boy—"*this!*"

There was a twinkle in his wife's eyes as she replied, "He was not so much of a horse—that one!"

"*Dumkopf!*" And the man went out slamming the door behind him.

Frau Carver laid her large hand on the little boy's head. His eyes were slowly filling with tears. It was true. He couldn't talk.

"Bah," she laughed. "He does not mean that. Quick now, make the fire. Once he has something in that stomach, all will be well."

And the clean, starched smell of her wide skirts filled his being with comfort.

The distant Ozark hills showed black against a faintly colored sky as Farmer Carver crossed the yard with its numerous outhouses and approached the huge barn. He sighed as he thought how empty it now was. He stamped his feet partly to keep them warm and partly because of the helpless rage. Of course, that child could help him very little, but what was he to do? Once he would have looked out over blue grass pasture land and a checkerboard of wheat and corn prairie. Once the large frame house of his nearest neighbor could not be seen for the thick orchard of fruit trees. But, now, the land itself seemed starved and beaten and only the smoked blackened ruins of his neighbor's house remained.

More than any other border state, Missouri had been torn and devastated by the War between the States. Since 1854 when an Act of Congress left the issue of slavery to be decided by the individual states, Kansas and Missouri had been caught in the struggle between free and slave states. Pro-Union and Pro-Southern groups made the war a peculiar horror. And the prosperous German farmers on the Ozark plateau suffered most. Hard-working, industrious immigrants, they had come to settle new homes in this land of plenty. The idea of slavery was abhorrent to them. When they needed extra help, they sometimes bought a few slaves and treated them as they were accustomed to treating hired help in Europe—as dependent members of their household. This attitude did not endear the German farmers to their slave-owning neighbors and when difficulties arose, it was upon the immigrants that their fury was lashed.

Moses Carver saw his land and ownings dwindle before the storm. He could not hire men to work his farm and he would not encourage the traffic of poor human beings, most of whom he suspected had been kidnapped.

At that time, Carver's wife had Mary, a soft-spoken, gentle slave girl, to help about the house. Mary's husband was owned on a huge plantation not many miles away. Often she had begged the German farmer to buy him, but George was a valuable slave, and his owner was a hard master. Sometimes weeks passed before George could get away to see his wife and three children. So it was a long time before they knew he was killed—falling from an ox team, they said. After that Mary was very silent, except at night when she sang her baby to sleep.

Farmer Carver's face softened as he looked across the field at the tumbled log cabin where Mary and her children had lived. Of course his wife was right. How could he expect that poor sick baby to work? He'd never be strong.

He struggled with the heavy barn door, finally getting it back upon its rusty hinges. His eyes fell upon the dust-covered harness hanging high above an empty stall. His anger stirred faintly again. But she had no right to say the horse was worthless! That he would not forgive!

Five years had passed since that bitter cold night when he had hurried home from the village, disturbed by that ominous notice: "Keep a careful watch on your slaves! Nightriders have crossed the border!" The settlers in Diamond Grove were bolting their doors and locking their gates with caution. Snatching slaves was more profitable than horse-thieving or rustling cattle. Though the War between the States was nearing an end, slaves still brought good prices in the markets of Arkansas and Texas.

When he reached home, Mary had already gone to her cabin. He heard her softly singing to her babies as he examined the latch. He had put his horse up, carefully bolting the door. Nightriders would take anything.

Susan had already heard the news and was worried. He spoke lightly of the whole matter.

"But I hear they crossed the river with some slaves," his wife said.

"Probably headed back the other way then."

"You can't be sure," Susan replied.

"Well, they'll not bother us. They can see I've got no slaves such as they want."

"Perhaps we'd better bring Mary and the children into the house to live," Frau Carver suggested.

"Oh, they'll be all right. The slavers are looking for men to work."

But he had been wrong. Late in the night he heard the scream. It was Mary. He grabbed his gun and ran out into the yard. But in the blackness he could see nothing. Only the galloping of horses and the slave woman's muffled cries came back to him out of the night. He rushed to the cabin. On the ground outside, her head bleeding, lay Mary's little girl. The little boy stood over his sister, whimpering. Inside, the cabin was empty. Mother and baby were gone!

By this time Frau Carver was calling.

There were no telephones in those days. It was several

hours later that Farmer Carver reached the village of Diamond Grove and rounded up help. He was not alone in his trouble. Several slaves had been stolen that night and soon a posse was formed. Farmer Carver could not go with them. The little slave girl had died before he left the house, and Frau Carver was almost hysterical. One of the women offered to return with him to her.

"Could we go back in your cart?" Farmer Carver asked. "My horse is faster than anything the nightriders have. I'd like to let one of the men ride fast on horseback to follow the raiders."

This was agreed upon.

"What shall we do if we catch up with them," asked one of the men. "They won't give up your slaves easily."

"Bargain with them," answered Farmer Carver. "My wife says we must get Mary back. I'm not a rich man, but I'll pay anything in reason."

"Did you bring money with you?" asked a second man.

Farmer Carver frowned. "No, and you'll need money. I'll tell you," he thought a moment, "give them the horse if necessary, but," he added quickly, "only if necessary. If they'll return, let them do so, and I'll pay them."

The men rode off. Days passed with no word. But nearly a week later they appeared at Farmer Carver's farm and told what had happened.

The nightriders had evaded them, thrown them off the trail and appeared gone. But the posse had waited at the border and finally they had come upon them trying to slip across. No shots were fired for fear of killing the slaves, and finally the thieves agreed to take the horse in exchange for the mother and baby.

"Tie him to a tree, retire out of sight. We'll examine the horse, and, when you hear us blow a horn, come and get your slave and her baby."

The men did not trust them, but a storm had come up and they realized they were at the mercy of the nightriders. So they had tied the horse to a tree and gone six hundred paces around the bend of the river. When they heard the horn it was far away and they knew that the nightriders had already put a mile or so between them. They dashed forward, found the baby soaking wet and shaking with cold on the ground by the tree, but the mother was nowhere about. The nightriders had tricked them and had taken her off with them.

When Frau Carver heard this story, tears had run down her cheeks. She had taken the dirty, soggy bundle in which lay the still form of the child. At first, they thought it was dead, but after a long time her tender ministrations brought some warmth back into the chilled frame. For days and weeks a racking cough choked the feeble breath until it seemed the baby could not live and even when life seemed promised, the baby's growth and development seemed stunted. But Frau Carver would not be discouraged.

"Mary's child must live—he will live!" She said it over and over again.

And at last, Mary's child did take a grip on life. He stood, he walked. He grew a little, but he could not speak. The violent cough, it seemed, had torn his vocal chords. Try as he might, he could not form words. Sometimes he uttered litle squeaking noises.

Of Mary they had never heard again. So all that they

had gotten for their valuable horse was this poor, weakened, speechless child. Farmer Carver shook his head dismally. What was he to do? He moved from one morning chore to another, hardly noticing that the sun was shining. Then he felt a gentle tug on his coat.

There beside him stood the little boy. He was smiling and pointing towards the house. Farmer Carver understood.

"So," he said heartily, "breakfast is ready. Well, I am ready for it. *Raus mit!*"

And taking the little brown hand in his, the big farmer strode across the yard. The little boy smiled happily. Frau Carver was right, as usual. The big man didn't mean it!

3. SECRETS OF THE WOODS

DAYS AND NIGHTS, weeks and months, merged and passed. The War between the States receded into history, slavery was gone and men set themselves to heal a ravaged country. Again, farmers could sow and reap their harvest, broken fences were repaired, and barns stood ready for the grain. Now, May had come once more among the Ozark hills. The valleys filled with warm mist in the mornings and all the earth was rich with promise. Wild crabapple trees bloomed white and pink, filling the air with perfume, patches of violets hid beneath soft mosses near the creek, and larks and thrushes called to one another in the woods.

These were wonderful days for a little boy whose ears caught every sound of growing things.

Frau Carver had a caller—a new neighbor but recently

come from far away Iowa and settled in the big, white house beyond the fields. Such good fortune, thought Frau Carver, her needles clicking happily. No longer would the afternoons and evenings be so long. Seated on the freshly painted front porch, Frau Carver bubbled over with information of all the surrounding country. Dull and unhappy enough these events had seemed during the years of conflict, but now the stories of hardships and night-riders were colorful and exciting to tell.

"And you never heard of that poor slave woman again?" asked Mrs. Mueller with deep sympathy.

"Never again," sighed Frau Carver. "The little girl died that same night. The boy and that poor, sick baby left. Ach, it was terrible!"

"What happened to the older one," asked the neighbor.

"He wandered away, after a while," replied Frau Carver.

"And after all the slaves were freed, what—" went on the woman.

"Shh! Here he comes now."

Through the trees at the side of the yard came the small dark barefoot boy, carefully carrying a large basket. He had grown a little in the past two years, but was still very thin and frail. He made his way between the garden plots and coming to a spot of finely raked soil, set the basket down gently and fell on his knees beside it. So intent was he that he had not glanced towards the porch.

"He's been to the woods and brought something back," informed Frau Carver. "This garden is his special care."

"It's such a lovely garden!" exclaimed the neighbor.

Up over the porch trellis climbed tiny red roses and

close to the house bloomed four-o'clocks and bachelor-buttons, while in well laid-out plots were dahlias and peonies and other flowers which Mrs. Mueller did not recognize. Beyond were rosebushes, each supported on a little frame. She watched the boy with interest. From the basket he was taking what appeared to be green-covered black dirt and, fitting the pieces of sod into the already prepared plot, was patting it gently with his hands.

"What on earth is he doing?"

Frau Carver laughed. "Perhaps I'll be able to answer that question later. He goes into the woods and gathers all sorts of mosses and wild flowers and replants them here. They always grow, but are usually different after he gets through working over them. Come, I'd like to show you one bed."

The two ladies laid aside their knitting and gathering up their skirts went down the porch steps and along the neat, gravel walk. The boy, absorbed in his work, did not notice them. As they approached they heard a low, murmur of sound coming from his lips. It was a crooning kind of song. Mrs. Mueller whispered,

"I thought you told me he was dumb!"

"He is—except for a few words. But he's singing to the flowers."

"Singing—," the lady began, astonished. Just then the boy looked up. He scrambled quickly to his feet.

"It's all right, George," said Frau Carver, "go on with your work. This is Mrs. Mueller. The Muellers have just moved into that big house down the road. I'm showing her your garden."

"It's beautiful, George!" Mrs. Mueller smiled at him.

George returned the smile shyly, then dropped back on his knees. But he continued to watch the two women as they passed down the path. He wondered if this new lady could really *see* flowers—or if, like most folks, she merely *looked* at them. He'd learned a lot about people in the past two years—certainly, that they couldn't see very well!

He sighed deeply. If only he could make them understand as easily as he did the wild things in the woods. Rabbits and squirrels and birds never minded because he couldn't make real words. In fact, he thought happily, they liked him just as he was. He was nearer their color, too, and they told him their secrets. They understood each other.

The two women were some distance from him now. He couldn't hear them, but he could see Frau Carver showing the lady those flowers the rabbit had led him to one day. He had made Frau Carver understand about the rabbit and how he had told him where they were. Frau Carver said he mustn't make up such stories, but she had laughed. Big people didn't seem to know that everything talked. *He* couldn't talk as well. It's true Frau Carver understood his squeaky, little sounds pretty well, but the farmer now— that was different. It was a good thing Frau Carver was around. He always stayed close to her! Take that time about the apple tree, for instance. *He* had seen those tiny bugs eating the tree away. The hired man, Farmer Carver, even Frau Carver, never saw them at all and they were working so hard to have a good harvest. He tried to show them to Farmer Carver, but the farmer had said,

"What do you want?" And then, "Go away, don't bother me!"

After he'd tried several times, he gave up. And yet, there were those bugs up there eating away. At last he had taken a saw, climbed up in the tree and started sawing away the branches where the bugs were. Mercy, what an awful row! The farmer pulled him down and was going to beat him until Frau Carver, hearing all the loud talk, came out. Then the boy, managing to pull away, ran to her and showed her the cut limb. He was breathless and shaking with fear, his voice squeaked worse than ever, but she knew immediately he was trying to tell them something important. And at last the farmer himself saw those tiny, crawling bugs. He never could understand how George knew they were there!

And yet, George remembered, Farmer Carver had read just that morning from the big book, "Lift up thine eyes!"

They had been calling him "George" for some time now, though Farmer Carver said it was ridiculous to call such a scrawny little boy after "Big George," as his father had been known.

"We've got to call him something," contended Frau Carver. "He can't grow up just 'boy.'"

His brother's name was Jim. He was much larger and had already wondered away from the Carver farm. He "hired out" doing odd jobs, returning occasionally and working in the fields, but offering little by way of companionship to the delicate, weak little George. They had explained to the boys that they were no longer slaves and could go freely anywhere they wished. But that meant nothing to George. Where would he go? Jim could not take care of himself.

At the edge of the farm under a tree was the little

mound where they said his sister was buried. George often slipped away and sat under the tree. He had planted green moss over it and encircled the mound with little colored stones. He thought his sister would like that. They were his very best stones, too. The cabin, also, was his—his and Jim's—that's what Frau Carver said. They told him about his mother, but he never could quite understand that. Was she dead? If so, where was her mound? He'd like to plant lovely flowers on it, too. For, after what Frau Carver had told him about her, he was sure she hadn't just gone off and left him and Jim. But when he begged Frau Carver to tell more, she had shook her head and her face was very sad. Then one day Frau Carver had said maybe she would come back. So he kept the cabin ready. Why should he want to go away? Even if Jim went, George thought he himself ought to stay.

There was much that George didn't understand. He seldom saw people except from a distance. The Carver farm was isolated and because he couldn't talk, Farmer Carver didn't allow him to go into town alone. Now that times were better and they had a cart, he would often ride in with Farmer Carver. From his place in the cart he observed all the wonders of the village and marveled greatly, but he did not leave the cart except to carry bundles, and then he walked close behind the big farmer. In town he saw other children, but they stared back at him, as speechless as he himself. So the little peoples of the woods were his only friends.

Now, he glanced up again at their visitor. He liked her face. He knew the big old house which had been empty as long as he could remember. Suddenly, he gave a start. The

pond! His brook! His fish house! He had just remembered
the stream running behind that very house and the little
pond he had built in it. Why—maybe he couldn't go there
any more now. And somebody might disturb his baby
fishes! He started up and then stopped, his eyes on the
basket. He'd have to finish. The delicate ferns would die
if left exposed like that. He looked up at the sky. The sun
was still high. He'd have time to finish the garden and
hurry across the fields and back before dark. He bent to
his task with renewed energy.

Meanwhile Frau Carver was proudly showing her
hyacinths.

"I never saw any like them," her visitor exclaimed.

"Nor have I," answered Frau Carver. "George brought
the tiny slips from the woods early in the spring. He's
tended them in his own way. Now I shall certainly let him
enlarge the bed, and next year I plan to enter them in our
flower show."

"But who taught him so much about flowers?"

Frau Carver shook her head. "Certainly not I. Let me
show you something else before I try to answer." Walking
to the edge of the path, she reached up into a young cherry
tree and held something out to Mrs. Mueller. "What
would you say this is?"

Mrs. Mueller took the object in her hand. "Why it's a
bird's nest. What kind of bird built it?"

"You see the tiny twigs, and leaves woven with chicken
feathers, hairs and soft mosses. Does it look different from
any other nest you ever saw?"

"No," laughed Mrs. Mueller, "I'm not good at this sort

of thing so it looks just like any other bird's nest to me. What's so different about it?"

"Only that *he* made it—not a bird!"

"What? You mean—"

"He says the birds showed him how to do it. What can I say? I know he watches every tiny animal—worms, bugs, lizards, and studies how they move. I've seen him lying for hours on his stomach watching an anthill. Every morning he looks in here to see whether or not a mother bird has made it her home. He'll be terribly disappointed if one doesn't."

She replaced the nest carefully on the limb.

"Well, I never!" exclaimed Mrs. Mueller, "but what has the nest to do with flowers?"

"Only that he says animals and flowers talk to him! That's how he knows what to do, he says."

"Oh, oh! What a story!" Mrs. Mueller was laughing heartily.

Frau Carver frowned a little. She did not like her neighbor to laugh at her queer little brown boy. She knew his stories were fantastic and yet—

"Come," she said hurriedly, "I'll show you the kitchen garden. It's quite as interesting." They passed around the house, but as they came out into the back yard Frau Carver exclaimed,

"Oh, dear!"

"Whatever is the matter?"

"That woodpile! You see it there?" Frau Carver's voice was distressed.

"Yes, it's very neatly piled. I wish I could get our Frank to—"

"Early this morning, before leaving, Mr. Carver told George to cut that wood. Here it is mid-afternoon and it isn't touched!"

"Oh, well, he's been busy in the garden. Can't he do the wood tomorrow? I don't think it will rain tonight."

"You don't understand, Mrs. Mueller. My husband is a stern man. He says George spends too much time now with flowers and idleness. We do want him to be smart and industrious, and he must obey."

"You're right. This boy will have a hard way to go in the world. He must learn to work."

"It isn't that he's lazy," defended Frau Carver. "Maybe," her face frightened, "maybe he didn't hear Mr. Carver tell him about the woodpile. I hope that was it—then he won't have to be whipped. Otherwise—" she shook her head.

"Well," laughed Mrs. Mueller, "if you're so anxious he'll not be whipped, he'll say he didn't hear, anyhow."

"Oh, no!" Frau Carver's voice was very serious. "George would never lie about it. I'll call him." She raised her voice, "George! George, come here!"

Around the house came George. He had just completed his gardening and he carried the empty basket. Now, he was ready to go to see about the pond. He stood waiting, his eyes on Frau Carver's face.

"George, did Mr. Carver tell you to chop this wood today?" Frau Carver's voice was very quiet.

In his dismay George dropped the basket. So that was it? The wood? How could he have forgotten! Not once during all the lovely May day had he thought about the wood. The pile loomed higher than anything he had ever seen. Oh, dear, oh, dear, oh, dear!

Frau Carver's voice was insisting. "Did he, George? Did you hear him tell you right after breakfast?"

Of course he had heard him—they'd stood right out there in the back and the Farmer had said very clearly, "I'll not be back until evening. Be sure this wood is cut by then." Oh, dear!

He looked at Frau Carver and nodded his head.

She looked very unhappy. "Why didn't you cut it?"

Then from his lips there came a flow of sound. The noises were like the chattering of some frightened, furred animal. He pointed to the basket, motioned with his hands. Frau Carver understood.

"Yes, you went into the woods for plants and forgot. You know what the farmer will do?"

George shivered slightly, his eyes filling with tears. How well he knew.

Frau Carver spoke briskly.

"Well, get at it at once! It's—it's not," she glanced at the sky, "maybe it's not too late. But, oh, George, do hurry!"

The two women quickly went into the house. George looked after them while black despair settled on his soul. Not for one moment did it enter his head that he might let the matter of the fishes go until morning. They were his baby fish—he was responsible for them. He had shut them up inside his fish house. Now perhaps they were in danger. Once he had caught a boy pulling one of the fish out on a string. The fish would have died! The boy ran away frightened out of his wits by the ferocious little dark bit of humanity which had leaped at him from the woods. Yes, he had to go and free those baby fishes. They were large enough now to take care of themselves, but not when they were hemmed in as he had them.

But—the woodpile! No matter how fast he ran to the pond and back, the sun would be down before he could get at that wood and Farmer Carver would certainly return long before it was finished. Farmer Carver would know he had not obeyed. And now even Frau Carver would not help him. She had told him to get at the wood immediately and he couldn't. He would be whipped. His stomach chilled at the thought.

Only a moment longer he stood. Then, swiftly across the field he darted. There was no choice. Come what may, he had to attend to his fishes!

Inside the house, Frau Carver was pouring tea.

She was really very proud of her little black boy. Not for one moment had he hesitated. She saw that Mrs. Mueller was impressed.

"Do you suppose your boy would ever have time to come over and get my flowers started?"

"I'm sure we could plan it, and I know George would love to do it."

"You call him George; what's his full name?" asked Mrs. Mueller, sipping the hot black tea.

"Slaves had no last name except their master's. Since this boy was born a slave, he has no other. We're not even sure his father's name was George. But it will do. You know, he's so sincere and honest all the time I've thought sometimes of calling him after that other little boy who would not tell a lie—George Washington."

"Oh, well, I don't think names make any difference anyhow."

"I'm not so sure of that," answered Frau Carver, thoughtfully, "and, somehow I feel that this name is just right—George Washington Carver."

"That's quite a name for such a little boy!"

"Who knows," mused Frau Carver, "perhaps God will bring him up to fit the name. God looks upon the heart."

4. MY FATHER'S BUSINESS

FARMER CARVER'S SPIRIT was that of the midwest pioneers. He would not be beaten by hardship. And now his farm began to prosper. He was far from rich, but again good crops were harvested, the barn was filled with golden corn and the huge smokehouse was full of meat.

Three years had passed. Boys born in slavery had no birthdays, but George must have been about ten that crisp fall morning when he tumbled off his cot so early. No one had to call him. Long before the old speckled rooster crowed for day, he was out in the barn, milking the cow, mixing the mush for the pigs, polishing the harness and feeding the horse. He paused here long enough to whisper in the mare's ear, "Eat well, so we can go fast—fast!" Then off to the chicken yard, passing as he went beneath the new grape arbors. There was a pleasant snap in the air and his handful of grapes were nicely chilled. Um-um, they were good! He sniffed the air, wrinkling his nose like a bunny. So many good smells—new-mown hay, ripe apples, corn shucks, heavy leaves, and now these luscious grapes!

The arbor was thick and the grapes plentiful. Farmer Carver had been dubious at first. Experiments could be expensive, but it had been hard to withstand the enthusiasm of the Swiss farmer, Hermann Jaegar. He had come from the next county and ridden up and down the countryside encouraging the farmers to raise grapes, had said the soil and climate was just right for them, had given away slips to start their vines. In George he had found an ardent disciple. It had been George who carried out the instructions; George who trained the vines along the frames; George who had kept them trimmed and watched carefully for any hungry bugs. Now, Farmer Carver was very glad he had decided to grow grapes and, because of them, special honor had come to this section of Missouri. The French government had bought cuttings from the grapevines of Hermann Jaegar. Learning that the French vineyards were being destroyed by phylloxera, or grape louse, this exile from his home vineyards had suggested to the French that they use cuttings and seeds from the wild grapes of the Ozarks as new roots for their vines. The offer was accepted. Now, Hermann Jaegar was told he was a patriot and France would use all the cuttings he could spare. And so the Ozark hills were transmitting their fresh, young sap to the worn-out vineyards of France and their vines were taking on new life and vigor.

It was to Farmer Jaegar's place many miles away that

George was going this morning. Since Farmer Carver had to go to the county seat, Neosho, he had decided to drive on over to visit the Swiss' fifty acres of vineyard. The idea of raising more grapes had occurred to him and so he decided to take George along to learn what he could.

"That boy picks ideas out of the air when it comes to growing things," he had confided to his wife.

"He certainly asks enough questions!"

Farmer Carver groaned. "Almost I wish he was not yet able to talk. This afternoon while helping me in the barn he asked 'Why is grass green? What makes grasshoppers jump? Why do morning glories fold up in the afternoon?' And, 'How long does it take to make a rainbow'?"

Frau Carver laughed. "So that's why you sent him in to me! Well, I'm glad. I finished my preserving at least an hour earlier, with his help."

"He's lots handier around a cook stove than he is with a plow," the farmer commented dryly.

"His growth is slow, but he's a smart boy." Then, his wife added thoughtfully, "He's nine or ten years old now and ought to be going to school."

Farmer Carver frowned. "There's no place for a colored child to go to school around here. What would he do with book learning?"

"He should know how to read and write."

The matter of George's schooling was dropped for the time being. But after supper Farmer Carver had said, "George, we're getting up extra early in the morning. I'm driving over to Newton County, and you can go with me to Hermann Jaegar's place."

"Oh! the grape man?" chirped George in his high, little voice.

Farmer Carver laughed. "Yes, that one."

The boy's eyes shone with excitement. He was silent a moment. Then, "Why are grapes purple?"

"I don't know," answered the farmer, while his wife looked on smiling over her mending. "All grapes are not purple, but nobody knows why some are purple and some —not." He turned away decisively.

George thought a moment and then asked, "Does God know?"

"Of course he does," answered the farmer devoutly.

"Then I'll ask Him," and George slipped quickly out of the room.

The farmer's face turned red. He opened his mouth to call, but Frau Carver laid her hand on his arm and spoke gently, "No, *mein Mann!* Let him go!"

"But—but—" protested the man, "it is not—right! He should not talk like that. Why—he sounded as if he were going to meet God out there—around the house!"

"Maybe he will," answered his wife quietly.

"Susan!"

He was lost in deep thought for a few minutes, then said, "You are right. He must learn to read. We cannot have a heathen growing up in our house. He must learn to read the Bible!"

"Mrs. Mueller gave him an old speller. He takes it with him every time he goes over there to work in her yard. She says he is learning every word in it."

"He must learn to read the Bible," repeated the stern

old farmer, who had been reared in the strict German-Lutheran church. "He must learn to *fear* God!"

George was a very happy boy as several hours later that morning he and Mr. Carver rolled along the dirt road approaching Neosho. George sat in the back of the cart, his bare feet hanging over the side. No one was concerned about George's appearance. He was just the Carver's "boy" and as such anything with which he covered his body was accepted as sufficient. The pants he had on once belonged to Farmer Carver. Simply by cutting off the worn legs and pulling a string about the upper part they were fitted to his slight frame. Mrs. Mueller had given him the coat. It had been left at her house by a visiting nephew, considerably larger than George. If the small boy made a grotesque figure no one cared, least of all he himself. As from a mighty chariot of state, he viewed the passing world and found it good.

Dog fennel, pennyroyal and goldenrod flamed in the fields. Trees touched with the breath of autumn wore their last party dress of gold and red. Purple hills rose in the distance and the sky was very blue. They passed apple orchards sweet with ripe apples and hay all stacked and ready for the barns. Negroes digging potatoes stopped to wave, and once a flock of geese waddled by. Many of the freed slaves had gone away, but here and there those remaining could be seen—"squatting" on a piece of poor land or living in bare cabins nearer the town, from which they went out to do odd jobs. The boy's vivid imagination pictured the interiors of those cabins from the one he knew—his mother's. He was keenly interested in the people living in them. He wondered why somebody didn't dig up the beautiful goldenrod growing along the side of the road and replant it in the cabin yards.

"Well, here we are in Neosho," called the farmer, looking back over his shoulder. "Better come up here on the seat with me."

George quickly climbed over the sacks of wheat piled in the cart and scrambled onto the narrow seat. He was glad because the many wagons, buggies and people passing along the streets frightened him, and he felt more secure close to the big farmer. Without realizing why, he shrank from the crude ugliness through which they were now passing.

Neosho had been a mining "boomtown" in the early days, serving the three lead mines in the vicinity. During the War Between the States, it had been the center of bitter fighting. In October, 1863, General Joseph Shelby attacked the Federal troops garrisoned within the courthouse, drove them out and burned the courthouse to the ground. For a long time rebellious guerrilla soldiers terrorized the neighborhood until, in 1866, order was established. But only one of the mines resumed work, sections of the town were abandoned, and the shacks fell in ruins. Recently a large flour mill had been opened and the town was beginning to take on renewed activity.

Their first stop was at the mill. The farmer went inside and George struggled with the heavy sacks of wheat until one of the mill hands, giving him a playful shove, sent the small boy sprawling in the gutter.

"Out of our way, beetle," said the man, laughing. "If one of these sacks fell on you, you'd be part of the flour!"

"And the flour would be *brown!*" called out another. At this they all laughed.

George picked himself up. His thoughts were confused. He realized the men did not want to hurt him—but how he wished he could carry the sacks easily! He wondered if small, weak black boys ever grew big and strong and whether or not they changed color so that they no longer differed from all the people who were doing things. From the way the men laughed it would seem that *brown* flour would be very bad indeed. He wondered why.

Soon the cart was emptied and they were off again. The streets were wider now and lined with big trees. Behind neat lawns sat painted houses. In the very center of the town a little park surrounded a large spring, after whose clear, cool water the Indians had named the early settlement. Here George climbed down to water the horse and, after a moment, Farmer Carver, taking his pipe from his mouth, remarked,

"This is a good place to eat our lunch, eh, George?"

Without waiting for a reply, he reached under the seat and took out the parcel Frau Carver had carefully placed there. Seating himself on the ground under a tree, he divided the contents and held out to George his portion. Frau Carver had known they would be hungry and the thick pieces of cornbread and boiled fat bacon were generous. The fact that the ear of corn was cold did not rob it of its good rich flavor, and as he ate George thought this was all very nice indeed. Village folk passing through the square observed the big white farmer and the very small dark boy sitting under the tree silently eating. When he had finished, Farmer Carver, still saying nothing, leaned against the tree trunk and looked up thoughtfully into its leaf-trimmed branches. George did not at all mind the farmer's long silences. Big people's talk to him usually consisted of orders which disturbed his observations. He was happier when they were silent.

An hour later they were crossing the White River. Never had he seen so much water and he leaned so far out trying to see everything that the farmer said sharply, "Careful there!"

George drew back into his seat, but he thought how wonderful it would be to sink down under that shining expanse. The thought of drowning did not occur to him.

The first sight of Hermann Jaegar's vineyards impressed even the stolid German farmer. And George held his breath. Row after row of vines on the hillside, and in the midst of lovely gardens, the great white house. Behind that house was something which caused George to stare— a glass house in which he could see green, growing things! Here they found Monsieur Jaeger, as he was known.

While the two men exchanged greetings, George slipped by and, fascinated, walked slowly between the benches. He had heard of Heaven. This, he thought, must be it! Timidly he extended his hand and touched delicate leaves. He caressed them with his fingers. He stopped before one box and began carefully to examine the earth, the tiny frames, the stems. Softly he spoke to them, saying how lovely they were and asking what they were. He did not know that he was singing. But Monsieur Jaeger had turned and, motioning Farmer Carver to silence, was listening.

"*Le petite noire*," he whispered, "*regardez-le!*"

Farmer Carver did not understand his exact words, but he did recognize his amazement.

"Yes," he answered, "he likes plants. He takes care of my grape arbors."

At this the Swiss farmer came up behind George and said softly, "*Mon enfant, vous—*" he stopped and then with some effort, "you—you love—plants?"

George looked up at him. Instantly there was a flash of understanding between them. Certainly, he could not have told how he knew, but he was certain that beyond all doubt here was a man who saw as he did.

"Yes—yes," he stretched his arms wide, "everything!"

"*C'est bien!*" the Swiss nodded his head. He took the little brown hand in his, flexing the fingers. "The hand of a gardener—his touch brings life." Patting the hand gently and letting it go he turned to Farmer Carver.

"*He* tended your grapes? But he is too small!"

In low tones, the farmer then told George's simple story —how his mother was stolen and how Frau Carver had cared for the sickly baby.

"He will never be strong. What will he do? Negroes can only work—and here he is now, freed, and unable to take care of himself." Farmer Carver shook his head sadly.

But Monsieur Jaegar again approached the boy, still busy examining the boxes. "Come," he said, smiling, "I will show you something about grapes."

Going to one of the boxes he explained, "Here are vines of wild grapes—I gathered them from the side of the hill and brought them here. The grapes are rather sour and small."

"But," interrupted George eagerly, "they are good. I

found some growing beside my creek." Then he added shyly, "Me and the rabbits like them very much."

The Swiss smiled, "Ah, yes, *petite*, you and the little creatures of the woods. God puts them there for you."

George gazed at him with wide eyes.

"And now," continued Monsieur Jaegar, pointing to another box, "here are grapes raised in Virginia. They are very sweet, but the vines are frail. They rot quickly and the grapes are pithy. Now, look carefully."

He broke a piece from each of the two vines, fastened them together and stuck the two slips into a third box which contained similar small double plants.

"Here, I bring the two together. The two produce one vine. I, Jaegar, work with God making better grapes. The wild vines are sturdy and strong; blended with the vines from Virginia they give—" he went to the door and with a sweeping gesture indicated the thick, green arbors, "grapes which we can ship to all the land!"

George's eyes were very round. This must be God, he was thinking, this kind man with his long black hair and swarthy face. But the man was still speaking.

"You see the hills and all the fields and all the hills and fields beyond—they belong to *Le bon Dieu*—all the earth belongs to God! And," now he was looking closely into the little boy's rapt face, "This God—this great God—is *your* Father."

"My—my—" the boy stammered.

"Yes, you are one of his little creatures—like all the small ones of the woods—you have no one else. But, see," he took the boy's hand again, "He has given you the grower's hand. You too must work with God, as I do!"

He turned away and after a moment George looked down at his hands, spreading the fingers and observing them closely for the first time. The "grower's hand" this wonderful man had said! Reaching into the box he let the loose dirt play through his fingers. And God was *his* father! But God had everything. He remembered Farmer Carver reading from the great Book. "The earth is the Lord's." He remembered the words well.

They turned their faces toward home late in the afternoon. Silently they watched the sun set behind the distant hills and saw the purple shadows fill the valley. Farmer Carver was thinking over this visit. New things had been shown him, things about cultivation of soil and planned crops. Much of the advice had come too late for his poor farm to benefit. He was growing old. Help was hard to get. He had no sons. He wished George were big enough to take over. But, with all his genius for growing things, George could not even plow.

George might have been asleep, he sat so still. But inside that tiny frame deep fires were kindling. Without being able to put it into words, he knew something very wonderful had happened to him that day.

After George had eaten such a meal as he did not dream could be, Monsieur Jaegar had come to him with an open book in his hand. Tears filled George's eyes as he shook his head. He recognized some of the words from his speller, but he could make no sense. The Swiss had only said,

"Take it. Already, you know much other people do not know—for you see more. But someday you will be able to read this book. You must read all the books. Then, your Father will teach you many things."

Now the book was hugged close inside George's ragged shirt. He had hardly dared peep at it.

As they returned through Neosho, Farmer Carver made one comment. "Herman Jaegar says there is a school here for colored children. You could go there."

George said nothing. Words were not necessary. The Carver farm no longer claimed him. From now on the earth was his—and, quickly, he must be about his Father's business.

5. AND HE JOURNEYED INTO A
FARR COUNTRY

ONE WEEK LATER George set out again on the road to
Neosho, this time on foot. When the farmer and his wife
had inquired about the school, they were informed that
the fall session was just beginning. Farmer Carver had
planned to take George to the school, but the night before
the calf had fallen sick and he could not leave. George
could not wait.

He had no school "outfit." But together, Frau Carver
and Mrs. Mueller had managed something that would do.
A pair of shoes, almost new, was his most prized possession.
They were much too good to wear on the dusty road, so
George had fastened the strings together and hung them
about his neck. The pants he had himself hemmed around
the bottom, and Frau Carver had cut down and fitted the
top. In an old, but thick, shawl she had tied up his belong-

ings, presenting him with the shawl for future use. In it were a good lunch, his spelling book, the precious book on plants given him by Monsieur Jaegar, a small knife which he used for trimming his plants, and two large apples. Nothing else, but tied in a rag about his neck was the first money George had ever owned.

The day before, when he had finished Mrs. Mueller's yard, she had said, "This time I pay you in cash. You'll need it for school."

And she had given him a handful of money. When Frau Carver had seen it, she had exclaimed. It amounted to a whole dollar! The school in Neosho for colored children charged a small fee, but everyone was certain this dollar would take care of his entrance.

He had no misgivings. Frau Carver had told him, "Go to some big house and tell them you can tend fires, cook and wash. Help is hard to get, and they will take you in."

The farmer said, "Remember, you are a free man. If they do not pay you something, leave. And when they do, guard your money well."

Frau Carver cautioned him about catching cold. "The shawl is warm," she said. "Wrap it well about you on cold nights."

Her heart ached for the little black boy. She knew something of what his struggle would be and yet she did not believe she ought to stop him.

She could not have done so had she tried.

As he reached the bend in the road he looked back. He was only ten years old, and he was leaving everything he knew. For one fleeting moment terror gripped him. Then the remembrance of his sweet secret returned. He looked out over the surrounding country—"The earth is the Lord's." He turned his back and sped down the road. Ten years were to pass before he saw the Carver farm again.

Years later, memory of what happened there was to be but faintly stamped on George's mind. He was to remember that those years had been very hard. But he was to recall that first night in Neosho when, foot-sore and weary, he crept into an old barn and fell asleep, his fingers holding fast to the paw of a large dog which laid down beside him.

The next day at school for the first time in his life he sat down in a room filled with other colored children. They stared at him. He was a stranger and his clothes were funny. He had put on his shoes and had carefully brushed the dust off his trousers, but he did not know that wisps of hay clung to his head. How they laughed when in his queer, piping voice he responded to the teacher's question with, "My name is George Washington Carver." And the titter that went round the room when he walked up and poured his money out on the teacher's desk!

He remembered how dumb he was.

When school was dismissed he sat waiting in his seat. He had not the slightest idea where to go. The teacher said roughly,

"Well, you there, get along home!"

He went out then and walked from house to house, saying what Frau Carver had told him. But nobody seemed to want as permanent "help" such a very little colored boy who could "make fires, cook and wash."

In the following days he did every imaginable odd job he could find—cutting wood, raking up yards, running errands. After the first couple of days he knew how to go to the store and buy a little food for himself. Once a man beat him because he thought he had been stealing apples. Each night after it was dark he would return to the barn, slipping out before dawn. And every day he went to school.

In later years he remembered vaguely that first terrible winter when several times he nearly froze to death. How he lived through it, why he didn't die for want of food and warm clothing, he was never able to explain. But live he did. The months passed and it was spring again.

At that time all schools for colored children let out early in the spring so that the boys and girls could help with the spring planting. George knew exactly what he was going to do when the school closed. He was learning, but the children still avoided him and the teacher made no effort to understand "that half-wit," as he called him. The thought that now he could read his precious book sustained George through many a hard and bitter day—days which he was not sorry to see come to an end.

Early one spring morning he set out on the road for Hermann Jaegar's vineyards. He was sure he could get work there. Many times the temptation to steal out to the vineyards had been strong, but the acres were miles away from school. So he had set himself to a task, and even on Saturdays and Sundays he had remained nearby working within sight of the school building. Now, he looked forward to weeks of happiness among the plants he loved so well and with the man who stood next to God in his mind.

When the big house came into view, he could have shouted for joy. The moment he was within the gate he could no longer walk, but ran towards the greenhouse. There he stopped. A strange man stood in the doorway.

"What d'you want, boy?"

The stranger saw only a painfully thin, ragged colored boy who stood now, his mouth open as if unable to speak. The man was busy. He repeated,

"What d'you want?"

When the boy did speak, the man could scarcely understand and the high piping voice irritated him. Certainly, this ragamuffin was stupid. He had to be told several times,

"*No, he isn't here.* Monsieur Jaegar is dead—yes, I said —*dead!*"

It was some time before George could really comprehend what the man was saying. A roaring in his head seemed to drown the voice. At last he knew. Hermann Jaegar had died during the hard winter. The fine vineyards belonged to someone else. No, the stranger didn't see how he could use a boy.

George was never able to remember how he got back to town. Searing pain blotted out everything. It may have been one day or several days later that he was awakened by a boot prodding him in the side. He rolled over, realizing that at last he had been caught sleeping in the barn. He expected the man to beat him, and because he was worn and tired and hungry and utterly discouraged he began to cry wildly. But the man leaning down only pulled him to his feet and shaking him gently said,

"Stop, stop—I'm not going to hurt you? Who are you? What are you doing here?"

When the boy managed to gasp out a few sentences the man said quietly, "Never mind any more—come with me!"

His tone was reassuring, and, still sobbing, George followed him. A little later George sat down at a clean kitchen table before the first real meal he had had in many months. While he ate, the man spoke quietly to his wife, who stood by watching.

Once she whispered, "He's starving—the poor little fellow!"

When George was fed, they showed him to a cot in the back shed and told him to lie down and rest. He fell asleep almost immediately.

And so George came to live with the Martins.

They were a young couple who had moved to Neosho with the opening of the new flour mill where John Martin was foreman. John's father owned a farm on the banks of the Ohio River and Lucy, his wife, had grown up in the little town of Oberlin. Both had seen many runaway slaves. Their sympathies had been deep for the poor black people and they had thought that emancipation would mean prosperity and plenty for them. Now here was a poor freedman, picked up half-starved at their very doorstep. They did not hesitate for a moment. And, though they did not dream it then, they were to bless that day.

When George realized this was to be his home—that he could keep the cot—when the shed was cleared and a little table put in for his books and papers, his joy was boundless. Vigorously he scrubbed himself that night out on the back porch. His old clothes were burned and cast-offs of John's pressed into service. To the boy they seemed raiment fit for a king!

He had told them all he knew about himself. Only of

Hermann Jaegar he did not speak—nor did he show them his book.

Early the next morning the Martins had their first surprise. Mr. Martin had to be at work by seven o'clock. He always made the kitchen fire the moment he was out of bed. And while he dressed, his wife prepared breakfast. But this morning he awoke drowsily from a pleasant dream of golden wheat cakes and delicious coffee. He stretched lazily before he realized that he *did* smell coffee. Lucy still slept peacefully on the other side of the bed. He sniffed again. There was no mistake. In fact, now came the rich aroma of frying bacon!

He sprang out of bed and hurried to the kitchen. There was George, humming happily, leaning over the hot stove, flipping wheat cakes!

"Good morning, sir," he piped.

Mr. Martin stared. There was no doubt about it. The bacon was fried to a turn—the cakes were golden brown!

"Where on earth did you learn to cook?"

"Oh, I cooked all the time with Frau Carver. She told me to tell anyone I can cook. See!"

Mr. Martin saw.

"I can wash, too," modestly added George.

"Well, I say!"

And so life began anew for the three of them. When John Martin had gone to his work, George insisted that little Mrs. Martin gather all the soiled clothes so that he could prove his boast. George observed the pile disdainfully. The pile was so small, and the clothes were not dirty! In a little while the line outside was blowing with snow-white sheets and curtains and towels. The German housewife had taught George well. He could wash!

The next day he spaded up the yard and begged for seed. Every day he thought of something new until the Martins urged him to go out and earn money for himself. They had no money with which to pay him for all he was doing, and soon it would be time for school and he would have nothing.

So, finally, each morning he would help with breakfast, wash the dishes, then strike out for jobs which took him into every part of the town. Now he was well fed, happy and secure. People no longer turned him away. He was in demand.

And he made friends and no longer avoided people. John Martin was very different from the quiet German farmer. He encouraged the boy to talk, tried to answer his questions and asked questions of the boy.

"He's sharp as a tack," John said one day to his wife, "but some things worry me a little. He doesn't yet know any colored people and he spends no time playing with boys. He's going to be much too old for his years."

His wife thought a moment. "I'll tell you: there's a colored church at the edge of town. Why not take him there some Sunday?"

"Better yet," agreed her husband, "why not let him go alone? Maybe he'll fall in with some of the boys and they'll get to know each other."

And so that night after supper Mrs. Martin said, "George, wouldn't you like to go to church Sunday?"

George, who was sitting on the edge of the porch shaping a piece of wood with his knife, looked up. "To church?" he asked. After a moment's thought, "What do they do there?"

"It's God's house, you know," answered little Mrs. Martin.

"God doesn't stay in a house. The whole earth is His," George spoke politely, but very firmly.

Mr. Martin was interested. He commented, "Yes, but people go to church to worship Him."

"Why? It's much nicer in the woods than in a house."

There was a moment's silence. Then the man said gently, "I'm sure you would enjoy the singing and you would see lots of people."

George smiled up at him. "Do you want me to go?" he asked.

"I think you'll like it, and yes—I think it would be good for you."

So the following Sunday, George, very clean and carefully brushed, went to church. He found his way easily, but hesitated just outside the door. Colored people were no longer strangers to him, but he did stare at their Sunday bonnets and bright dresses. He did not have on "store-bought" clothes as did some of the boys, but he was not conspicuously different, and he was able to slip in unnoticed and take his place on the back seat. Then the singing started and he forgot everything else. Deep within him stirred some faint memory. He had heard those songs before. He was sure of it. He sat entranced.

He did not like the sermon which followed. He did not think the man could know God very well, not nearly so well as Hermann Jaegar. The shouting frightened him.

And he felt no particular kinship with the several people who spoke to him after the service, "You the little boy works over at Mis' Thompson?" "What's your name, boy?"

One boy who had laughed at him in school now said, "Hi, there!" He answered everyone's greeting politely. But the two little girls who giggled at him he thought very silly.

Then, he saw a Personage approaching! People bowed respectfully and gave way for "Aunt Mariah" Watkins. He heard them greet her.

"Howdy, Aunt Mariah!"

"Hope you well!"

"As th' Lord wills, mah Sister. As th' Lord wills!" was her answer.

George stared. She did not look like Frau Carver, but once more he seemed to smell the starchy freshness of Frau Carver's billowing skirts.

For Aunt Mariah was so clean!

The black-and-white print dress bristled with cleanness. Across her shoulders was a snow-white shawl, above which shone her large and kindly face, the black skin smooth and free from blemish as a baby's. And on her head a stiff and glistening bonnet. She paused a minute, with a pearly smile for the small stranger.

"Yo' all by yo'self, son?"

So many colored children in those days after the War Between the States were all alone, and Aunt Mariah's voice was gentle.

"Yessum—I—" George began to stammer.

"Nice manners, too," commented Aunt Mariah. "Well,

not a sparrow falls that th' Creator does not know—an' yo' much bigger den a sparrow!" Then she was gone.

George looked after her, wishing—he hardly knew what wish was in his mind. She was like—a cool—shady tree—under which he'd like to lie! That was it. He smiled, thinking how silly the thought was.

On his way home he wondered about what he should tell the Martins. All things considered, he decided he didn't care much for church. He wished he could hear the singing out under the trees. To the end of his days, he preferred God's great outdoors.

They did not insist on George's attending church regularly. But they were interested that he had been so attracted by the lovely music. Oddly enough he didn't mention Aunt Mariah. He wasn't sure they'd understand. They might think he was laughing at her, and he wasn't—so he was silent.

Some Sundays, after that, he would cross the railroad tracks near the church and stretching under some tree, listen to the singing. Several times he caught a glimpse of Aunt Mariah. That always made him feel good.

John Martin made one more attempt to develop George's social life. By this time everyone knew of the boy's industry and thoroughness with his work and he was well liked by the neighbors. One afternoon John heard that some of the neighborhood boys were going fishing the next morning and he urged them to ask George to go along. George seemed very pleased with the invitation and they all set out about dawn. Later, the boys told John Martin what happened.

"All the way out to the river, he was fine," one of them started, "but—"

"He's crazy, Mr. Martin, honest!" the second boy interrupted.

"He started yelling when we took out the worms to put on our hooks."

"He grabbed our worms away and stuffed them in his pocket!"

"We tried to show him how the fish bite down on the worm and is caught on the hook and—"

"He got awful mad!"

"He said God would punish us for killing the fish!"

"He ran off into the woods and wouldn't come back!"

John tried no more. For the remainder of the summer when George wasn't working, he assisted Mrs. Martin about the house, tended his garden, or sat idly on the porch whittling his sticks.

Then it was time to return to the one-room school. Now George learned quickly. He was no longer strange to the other boys and girls. While they continued to regard him as odd, they no longer laughed at him.

The weeks passed quickly until that bitter cold night in February when Mrs. Martin became very ill. George ran for the doctor, built a fire, heated water, and stood anxiously by, ready to answer calls. For days they thought she would die, but the danger passed and she started on the long, slow road towards recovery. George did not return to school. He was nurse, cook and housekeeper. He made Mrs. Martin laugh at his antics. During those days he developed a wit and ability for mimicry which never left him. Each morning John Martin would go to work amazed at his good fortune in having George in the house. At night the tall white man and little black boy would work school problems, read and spell. It is quite likely that George's education advanced more rapidly than it would have in the school.

With the coming of spring Mrs. Martin regained her strength and she urged George to go out and make money for himself. Then came another blow. The flour mill shut down and Mr. Martin found himself without a job. An uncle wanted them to join him in California and after several futile attempts to find something in the vicinity, they decided to accept his offer.

George was their chief concern. They had so little money. The long illness with doctor bills had depleted their meager savings and with no certainty of immediate employment, Mr. Martin's future was insecure.

"How I wish we could send him back to Oberlin!" Mrs. Martin said several times. They had seen other freed children in that school and knew he would be welcomed.

"He'll not learn much more here," her husband declared.

"If he could get to Kansas! The schools are so much better."

But there was no money.

They told George about the schools of Kansas, that they were free to white and colored children alike. Kansas was sixty miles away. In those days that was a great distance.

Everybody in the little town soon knew the Martins were "going West." Another couple in the town of Grandby ten miles away heard the news and drove over to say they had been waiting to find a partner willing to share expense of a wagon and team of horses. They, too, were "going West." So the Martins made a bargain, and in the covered wagon the two families packed all their belongings. All the neighbors gathered to see them off. George knew that his friends were going on a long and dangerous trip and his heart was heavy that morning. They had made arrangements for him to stay with a neighbor. Everyone knew their high regard for George. But finally the wagon rolled away.

George stood in the doorway of the empty house. His throat was tight and everything in front of him a little blurred, so he did not see Aunt Mariah until she was directly in front of him. He blinked rapidly.

"I'm hyear to take yo'-all home." It was a simple statement.

"They said—they said"—George pointed across the fence.

"I knows," Aunt Mariah's voice was judicious. "They is mighty fine folks round here. Won't let no smart boy lak yo' be out in th' streets, but hit's high time yo' own lent a helpin' hand. Come 'long!"

She spied the pile of foodstuffs in a bag. "Is these-here yourn?"

"Yessum," George murmured. "Mis' Martin gave 'em to me." Potatoes, apples, corn and beans, a piece of bacon and some eggs—luxurious supplies for one small boy.

He stuffed his few other remaining belongings into the bag, and with it bulging on his back, he followed her. They crossed the tracks and came to a cabin just a few doors below the school. The houses over here were small. Aunt Mariah's was but a single room, very bare, yet the cleanliness of Aunt Mariah's person was reflected in her house. On the floor, smooth with many scrubbings, were rag rugs. There was no glass in the window openings, but she had stretched starched white netting across them. The yard was swept as clean as was the room, and not a blade of grass showed anywhere. Neatly arranged on a bench were the implements of her trade, washtubs and board. Inside, the room had a pleasant, aromatic odor of spices, pines and dried food.

Aunt Mariah showed George a cot in one corner behind a homemade screen. This was her "spare room," but now he would occupy it. She bustled about and soon set on the table a thick and savory stew.

Then he met Uncle Andy.

Had Andrew Watkins been born a white man, he would assuredly have been a "country gentleman," a "gentleman of leisure." Truly, he was one of "God's gentle men," soft of voice, courtly in manners, charming in every attitude. But—Uncle Andy drank! And so he never kept a steady job. The burden of the household fell upon Aunt Mariah's competent shoulders. She "took in washing" and faced the world with calm assurance.

It was to Uncle Andy that George talked of Hermann Jaegar. He read him portions of the precious books describing plants and flowers. He set about to make a little flower bed in the yard, and started a vine along the cabin wall. Uncle Andy was enchanted. He could read the Bible, a little. It had long been his and Aunt Mariah's custom to sit in the yard each evening before the light had gone, and Uncle Andy would read aloud. Now that George had come, with all his "learning," they handed the Bible to

him. At first he stammered and stumbled over the unac-
customed words, but gradually he found that certain parts
were just like singing. These sections became easy and
since his listeners did not seem to mind, he read them over
and over until they fastened in his memory. Aunt Mariah
and Uncle Andy would listen appreciatively and sometimes other neighbors stopped to hear.

> "The heavens declare the glory of God; and the firmament
> sheweth his handywork. Day unto day uttereth speech and
> night unto night sheweth knowledge. There is no speech nor
> language, their voice is not heard. Their line is gone out
> through all the earth, and their words to the end of the world.
> In them hath he set a tabernacle for the sun."

The light faded, but his voice went on. He knew the
lines. As they sat under a sky studded with stars, from the
darkness in the adjoining yard would come a voice, "Dat
boy read lak a angel!"

Aunt Mariah was proud. Looking fondly at George she
said, "Yo' sho reads wid th' spirit, George Washington.
Maybe yo' gonna be a preacher."

"Oh—no!" George cried in alarm. He didn't want to be
a preacher!

"Ah reckon he's gonna be a school teacher." Uncle
Andy could think of no higher praise.

"Well, preacher or school teacher—don't matter one or
t'other. Yo' gonna be *somethin'*. That's certain!"

And so George learned how three people can live together in one room, and how faith, hope and love can fill
that room.

George went to school, running home at recess time to

help Aunt Mariah with the huge piles of wash. Sometimes he'd bring a book and prop it up against a board so that he could study while he worked.

Months passed and George absorbed all this teacher could give him. The boy's discerning questions now irritated him. Clearly, the time had come for George to go somewhere else.

As he went about the town doing odd jobs, he began asking more questions about Kansas. Since before the War Between the States, Kansas had been a "promised land" to Negroes. It was called the "free state." So George heard glowing stories of abundant work and great cities, and the determination grew in his mind that he must go there. Hermann Jaegar had said, "You must read all books." He began to glimpse the task ahead of him. He must go where he could do exactly that.

When he talked it over with Aunt Mariah and Uncle Andy, Aunt Mariah said she would pray over it. Later she informed the boy that the Lord had told her not "to meddle."

"Yo' put your trust in Him and He will lead you."

She had taught him many things, had talked at length on "manners."

"Live humble, George. Folks what keeps their nose in the air gets some mighty hard falls!"

Uncle Andy was a little wistful. "Reckon yo' have to know a lot to be a school teacher," he said.

George tried to explain. "I want to—make—things, Uncle Andy."

"Like what?"

"Well—" George hesitated. He drew out a piece of

wood upon which he had been whittling the evening before. "Like this—only—much—" He didn't finish.

Uncle Andy examined the wood. It was a rose, carved out of wood, each petal distinct. He handed it back and nodded. "You *powerful* smart!"

So early one morning George set out for Fort School. He left the kind couple most reluctantly, but in his heart he was very sure that the Fort School was his next stop. The school was in Fort Scott, a former military outpost on the south bank of the Marmaton River, five miles west of the Missouri line.

He was still small and thin, but his legs were now wiry and tough. He could read and write and figure. He felt very much a man. Furthermore, he now carried a neatly folded package of belongings, a good substantial lunch and several dollars. And in the center of the bundle was Aunt Mariah's parting gift—a brand new Bible.

A few miles out from town a mule team overtook him. One of the men driving recognized him and told him to jump in. He scrambled up into the cart and began the second lap of his journey.

6. SEARCHING FOR WISDOM

THE WILDER HOUSE, facing the Plaza on Main Street, was the busiest corner in Fort Scott. Here the tri-weekly stagecoach from Kansas City drew up with a great flourish and discharged its well-dressed passengers. Here rough-riding cattlemen met ranchers from all parts of the West and the townsmen stopped for a cooling drink and remained engaged in heated discussion. There was constant coming and going, much loud talk, laughter and frequent fights. Yes, a wide-awake, cheerful colored boy could find much to do in such a spot.

It did not take George long to discover the Wilder House, nor the Wilder House long to discover George. Kansas was booming and energetic workers were needed. Before many weeks George was established in one of the outhouses behind the hotel, running his own "business." He had started as helper with the hotel wash, but so efficient did he prove that soon he was doing all of it. This gave him an idea. Steam laundries did not exist. Travelers were glad to have someone pick up their soiled linens and return them clean and fresh. George made money.

He was an asset to the hotel and so was allowed to have a cot on the back porch. The cook became his friend and ally. Long before it was time to start her day's work, he had emptied ashes, made fires in the huge stoves, heated water and carried the heavy steaming pails out to his sheds. On busy days, after the arrival of the stagecoach when she was rushed, he'd help with the cooking. She saw to it that he had something to eat.

"You do not eat enough," she would grumble. "All that washing and ironing—you are too small!"

Yes, George was small for his thirteen years. He had to stand on a little stool to reach the tubs. But he enjoyed plunging his arms into the steaming suds. He'd attack a soiled garment with ruthless fury and the dirt would fly. When it was smoothly ironed and carefully folded, George viewed his finished product with all the instinctive pleasure of the artist. He had transformed ugliness to beauty!

By the time he presented himself at the brick school on the square, he was already known by one of the teachers, and several of the children's parents had given him work. The building was large, with many rooms, and George stood hesitating in the hall. In spite of what he had been told, it did not seem possible that he could go to school here.

"Are you entering school, little boy?"

He looked up into the face of a young woman who

reminded him of Mrs. Martin. She smiled at him, thoroughly understanding his shyness. She had seen other colored children timidly standing on the threshold of this school, but none quite so thin, none so poorly dressed, none so eager as this boy. She found that he could hardly talk at all. Speech was still very difficult for him. And when he was nervous or excited, stammering rendered him totally incoherent. But she was very patient. He finally made himself understood and she led him to her classroom.

At first it was impossible to assign him to a grade. He could read and spell very well. He knew little arithmetic, but he learned it quickly. He could hardly write at all and he knew nothing about geography or history. But in the Nature class he amazed the teacher and told her many things she did not know.

Now every moment of his day was filled to overflowing. His determination carried him forward. He began to read everything he could get his hands on. His teachers lent him books, he picked up newspapers about the hotel, he listened to the talk of travelers and he forgot nothing.

Frequently George was homesick for the woods and the "little people" who inhabited them. He longed for a flower garden. But there was no time for anything except his work and school. When the longing became too great, he satisfied it by drawing pictures on scraps of paper. He drew trees, brooks, rabbits, squirrels, and flowers—anything which he happened to be visualizing. Sometimes he would save the paper and stick it away in the back of his desk, in a book or under his cot. These pictures seemed to bring the objects back to him. He had not lost them.

One day the teacher interrupted her geography class to

ask rather sharply, "George Washington, what are you doing?"

For some moments, she had noticed that George was paying no attention to the lesson. She had been surprised and had endeavored to recapture his attention without calling his name. But he had continued to stare out the window, until he became busy over a piece of paper, his book lying face down on the desk. At her question, George looked up, startled. He had heard his name, but it was evident his mind was far away.

Just before he had become so inattentive, the class had been talking about "mountains and hills." Suddenly, George had seen the hills behind Hermann Jaegar's house. Once more he was standing in the green-house doorway and he seemed to hear Hermann Jaegar saying, "Lift up your eyes to the hills—" Almost without realizing it his pencil began to trace those lifting hills, with their vineyards—the mountains rising in the distance and—

Now he stared at the teacher stupidly and asked, "Ma'am?"

The children tittered.

"What do you have there?" the teacher asked.

George looked down at the sheet of paper. The spell was broken. He saw only some broken lines. The hills had disappeared.

"I—I—" he began to stammer.

"Bring me that paper." The teacher's tone was positive. Reluctantly George went forward and laid the sheet on her desk.

She studied it a moment without speaking. Then she asked, "Where did you see these hills?"

He tried to answer, but could not speak. She waited patiently. He was remembering the geography lesson of several days ago and finally managed to stammer—

"O-zark . . . Ozark—foot—hills!"

"Yes, I thought that was what they were." The teacher spoke naturally, endeavoring to quiet his nervousness. "They were near your home?"

The boy nodded. For one brief moment the awful sense of bereavement which he had suffered by Hermann Jaegar's death engulfed him. His eyes filled with tears.

"This is a very good drawing—very good indeed," the teacher was saying, gently. "Will you stay a few minutes after school?"

As George returned to his seat, he felt disgraced. He was being kept after school! The other children regarded him wide-eyed, some with sympathy, others with speculation.

But as soon as the room was cleared, the teacher went to George's desk and asked if he had any other drawings. He produced a few from behind his books. He thought she was going to punish him by taking them away, but when she had looked them over carefully she handed them back and said,

"You should be in Miss Long's drawing class. I'll speak to her about it."

Now George smiled. It was evident she liked his pictures.

"I—I—have some more," he ventured shyly.

"You have? Bring them tomorrow and we'll show them all to her. I know she will be glad to have you for a pupil!

Now run along, and," she smiled at him, "don't work too hard!"

It was not long before George was Miss Long's star pupil. And when, at Christmas time she gave him a box of water colors, in all the world there was no happier boy!

Three years passed rapidly. George was in the upper classes now and school was about to close for the summer.

Men stopping at the Wilder House talked excitedly of swarms of grasshoppers which had come out of the West and ruined the crops in Iowa. Kansas farmers thanked God devoutedly that they had not come further south, then went on to talk of a new railroad being laid from Kansas City to a far-off place in Colorado called Denver. There were stories of Indians along the southern border and of wild happenings in Texas.

All this stirred George's vivid imagination. "The earth is the Lord's"—all the earth! These far-distant places— deserts—high mountains and great rivers. Why not see more of this wonderful earth? He thought of the Martins and wondered how they had liked California. Now that he knew of California's warm climate and abundant sunshine he was glad frail little Mrs. Martin had gone there. The West was expanding. Railroads and bridges were being built. More men were needed.

So it was that one day there came to the Wilder House a man signing up laborers for the new railroad. Without hesitating he took George's dollar, and, signing his name, gave him a card telling him where to report in Kansas City. The hotel people warned him the work would be too hard, the men coarse. But George was sure he could take care of himself and the wages were excellent.

He traveled in style, by stagecoach, to his new job. Long since the country people had coined a phrase for the stage fare to Kansas City—"Ten dollars and carry a rail,"—indicating that the passenger must walk alongside the stagecoach when the road was bad. Passengers usually had to walk about one-third of the way, often putting their shoulders to the wheel while the horses strained pulling the coach out of deep mud. But George felt himself quite able to do his part whenever necessary, as they rolled over the rough roads.

He did not risk losing himself in the big city when they arrived, but immediately followed instructions and found the construction building. A dozen or so workmen were standing in line. They stared at the small dark boy when he took his place with them. The man at the desk, paying no attention, was copying his name from the card which he had laid before him when he happened to glance up.

Then he exclaimed, "Hey, wait a minute. We're not taking kids!"

Looking at the card he asked, "Are *you* George Washington Carver?"

"Yes, sir. I—" began George in his high, childish voice.

"Anybody with you?"

"No, sir, but—"

"You won't do at all. You're much too small," the man declared.

George's heart fell. Then he said quickly, "I can cook."

"Oh, I see, you're one of the helpers. Why didn't you say so? All right, stand over there."

A couple of hours later George was in a covered wagon with about twenty men, headed west. They traveled for several days, stopping at night to throw themselves on the ground and sleep. For the most part they were silent men and addressed few words to the quiet little boy. As the expanse of western prairie unrolled before him, George was glad he had come. The cloudless blue sky was like a huge inverted bowl, studded at night with blinking stars. The boy lay on his back gazing up at them. He breathed deeply and felt the cool, clean air lifting his lungs.

"This is good!" he thought happily.

When they arrived at the large construction camp, George was directed to the cooking crew. These men worked over open fires, roasting meat on spits and swinging big pots over the flames. When the contents were done, the pots were set on the ground and the cooks dipped ladles into them, pouring the steaming mixtures into bowls held by the line of hungry workers. This was not always easy for a small boy to manage, and if he was slow or spilt hot food he was likely to be burned or be soundly cuffed on the head. Then there were horses to be watered and fed, refuse to bury and piles of dishes to wash. George earned his money.

Then mid-summer came. All day long the scorching sun beat down. There was no relief. The men worked and lived outdoors and there were no trees. As George trudged up and down the tracks with his water pail and dipper, he tried to forget the heat by thinking of leafy trees, damp green mosses growing beside brooks, and cooling rains. Sometimes he succeeded. And the nights were a joy. For when the sun had sunk blazing into the earth, there came a wave of cool air. The men lay prone upon the ground and slept.

George had signed up only for the summer. At the end of the three months he collected his money—more than he had ever had before—and struck off, not east, but west. He wanted to know what lay beyond. He wanted to see the mountains. He wanted to become better acquainted with his "Father's" world.

For a while he cooked at a ranch. Then, meeting a group of fruit pickers going south, he joined them. The strange plant life of New Mexico fascinated him. He spent hours gathering desert flowers. The long exposure to the sun, release from hard work and this continued period of living outdoors combined to pour new life into George's frail body. A little later he was to shoot up like those sturdy desert plants which puzzled him.

One evening just at sunset he came across a plant stranger than anything he had ever seen. It was very large and seemed to grow right out of the sand. He walked around it examining the hard, thorny leaves. Then, tearing a strip from a bag of fruit he was carrying, he lay down flat on the sand and sketched the outlines.

Fifteen years later his finished painting of this plant was to receive honorable mention at the World's Columbian Exposition in Chicago. The plant had been identified as a rare species of Angustifolia Yucca with cactus growing beside it.

When the first hint of fall coolness touched the air, George started back to Kansas. Schoolhouses were scarce in that wild cactus country and George knew that school was what he wanted.

He had not intended to stop at Olathe, Kansas, but the brightly colored barber pole caught his eye. It was like a huge stick of peppermint candy topped off with a gleaming golden ball. Then, behind the shining window he saw the sign "Boy Wanted." He went in.

"Big Nat" looked up quickly, expecting another customer. He frowned slightly when he saw the gangling, shabby figure, nodded his head, but resumed his story as he carefully snipped a few more hairs from the massive beard under his hands.

"Yessuh," his big voice boomed, "that there cyclone picked up tha barn, carried hit two miles an' put hit right down in ole man Ganger's front yard . . . an' tha hen still settin'!"

The customer, stretched out in the chair, lifted his head, "No!" his amazement was evident.

"Eggs hatched out tha next day," the barber nodded, "not a chick lost!" He waved the scissors in mid-air and stepped back studying the beard.

The customer blinked at George.

"Want a shave, son?"

Big Nat's brown face lighted up with a grin. He loved a joke.

"No, sir," George's high voice startled the two men, "I'm looking for a job."

"Oh!"

Both men looked him over intently, their faces serious.

"What can you do?" asked the barber.

"Anything you want done?"

They approved the utter confidence in the tone, but Nat regarded the newcomer dubiously. However, it was Saturday. Soon his place would be crowded with ranchers and townsmen. He needed a helper badly. So George was hired.

That night George slept on a packing box in the back of the shop. He awoke at dawn, his head aching. After his nights in the open, in barns and hay lofts the heavy, smoke-laden, close air of the barbership stifled him. He sat up gasping. He had to get out. Then he remembered it was Sunday. The shop would be closed and he was free. That realization brought visions of a creek he had passed the day before as he entered the town. He would go swimming, remove the grime and dirt of the road and start the day off right. In his pack was his "other" shirt, which was clean. Taking a towel, a bit of soap and tucking the shirt under his arm he unlocked the door and stepped out into the sweet, morning air. He felt rather important as he fastened the door behind him and pocketed the key. Big Nat had expressed his confidence in him and he liked the towering barber.

The town was just beginning to stir. Sunday was the one morning Kansas menfolks could lie abed after the sun came up. True, the boys had to get up and go out to feed chicken and hogs. And the girls must go down into the big kitchens to assist their mothers with the hearty Sunday morning breakfast. Young folks didn't stay in bed after sunrise, unless they were sick.

As George hurried along the road and approached the creek he was thinking of Aunt Mariah and her frequent admonition, "God put watah on dis earth to use—inside and out!" He remembered her hard "scrubbings," as he tossed off his coat and trousers and slipped into the clear, cold water.

He stayed until the pangs of hunger brought his mind to the immediate problems. He had some money, but where was he to eat? Big Nat had been so busy the day before that they had discussed no details. He had shared his lunch with the new boy and when he left the shop had indicated that he could spend the night there. George had seen several eating places in the town, but he knew by bitter experience that a colored boy could not just walk into any place, even though he had the money to pay. As he pulled on his clothes, he knew he must find food and that quickly.

He decided to take a short cut across town and as he suddenly turned a corner around a grove of trees he stopped—his hunger vanished! For George was facing a white house and yard that made him forget everything. He walked slowly toward it, his eyes rapt. This might have been *his* yard—green grass, and morning glories, their faces lifted to the sun, a mass of goldenrod and tulips, in a carefully bedded center plot. He pushed open the gate of the white-washed, picket fence and went in, not for a moment considering himself an intruder. The flowers had called to him. He was at home.

And so Aunt Lucy Seymour found him, crooning over her flowers. When she spoke to him he began immediately telling her why the hyacinths were not doing better. He asked for scissors to trim the roses and while he sat in the kitchen eating the breakfast she set before him, he told her of a lovely moss he had seen beside the creek that morning and offered to transplant it to the yard.

Aunt Lucy was from Virginia. She had belonged to one of the "first families" of that state and considered herself infinitely superior to other colored people who had stemmed from less exalted station. She believed in "blood." Though she and "Uncle" Seymour had struck out for themselves with western bound pioneers, she had endeavored to bring a little of the emerald greenness of her native state into the bare, wide-open space of Kansas. She shrank from the naked ugliness of weather-stained, unpainted houses and yards swept clean of every blade of grass. Now, her heart warmed to this ragged, clear-eyed boy who touched her flowers so tenderly with such "knowing" fingers. She said instantly that George had "good blood in his veins!"

Whereupon George went to live with Aunt Lucy and Uncle Seymour. Much of the stern, Presbyterian creed of the devoutly religious Uncle Seymour sank into the boy's mind and heart. Aunt Lucy stood for no "foolishness." In her beaded, silk dress with its high-boned collar, long full skirts, her black lace gloves and with her fan she was every inch an "aristocrat." Early Monday morning she donned a starched gingham dress and over tub and board turned out the finest laundry in the county. People from other towns brought their white organdies and fluted laces to her. To her they brought dainty bodices with fine-seamed tucks, each one to be ironed so carefully, and fancy underskirts with handwork and lace so exquisite it seemed a shame they were not seen. She took pride in her work.

They had no children and as time passed their pride

enveloped George. George was not an added burden. He went to school, worked evenings and Saturdays in the barbershop and yet found time to help Aunt Lucy and to improve the yard. When the Seymours moved to Minneapolis, Kansas, George accompanied them. The schools there were better, offering him high school. The town grew and the laundry business prospered.

During these years of wandering, George had had little communication with those he had left behind. His days were too full, his mind taken up with daily necessities, his eyes fixed on goals ahead. His brother Jim had been dead over a year before he knew about it. Jim had died of smallpox and been buried in Fayetteville, Arkansas. George's throat contracted with pain as he realized that the vague dream of his brother and himself someday "walking together" was forever gone. Though he knew so little of the details of Jim's life, he could imagine much. They had been two small Negro boys, tossed like wreckage out of the great sea of slavery, hardship and poverty— no parents, no home, no background, no anchor. One of them sank down upon the shore and the waves of oblivion had washed him back into the sea. The other had turned his face towards the mountains!

George finished high school at Minneapolis. He did not take part in the school graduation, but decided to celebrate the event by going back to see the Carvers. He wanted once more to visit his mother's cabin, to run through those woods, to tell the farmer and his wife what he had done. He knew they were getting old now and that they would be very happy to know he had come this far along his way. Aunt Lucy helped him to get ready. This trip was a real event. He had been working in a restaurant and had saved some money. Now, he bought presents for the farmer and Frau Carver and boarded the train with high anticipation. Except for the great lines going east and west, there were few railroads then in this section of the country. George, who had never been on a train before, did not purchase his ticket before getting on.

When the conductor came down the aisle, he looked at him and asked, "Where you going, boy?"

"To Diamond Grove, Missouri," piped George in his queer, little-boy voice.

The conductor shook his head.

"Nope! I can't be looking after children. That's too long a trip for a little boy like you to make alone."

George smiled and drew the fare from his pocket. "But I'm not a little boy. I've just finished high school, and I can take care of myself."

The conductor was doubtful, but George had spoken with quiet assurance. The man liked this neat little colored boy, and whatever his age, he decided to help him.

So he said, "Well, you can ride for half-fare."

This amused George, but he stuffed the extra money back in his pocket, glad that he would have more than he had thought when he arrived.

The Carvers welcomed George as if he had been a long-lost member of the family. The news of his return spread through the countryside and many were the visitors who listened as he told of where he had been and what he had been doing. They were all proud of this young Negro and wanted him to know that they appreciated his struggles.

They marveled at his learning. He showed Frau Carver how food was cooked in restaurants, at the hotel and in the camp. He prepared delicious meals and even taught Mrs. Carver to cook Mexican dishes. He demonstrated how he ran his "laundry" by doing all the wash in a short time. Then, going out with Farmer Carver to the barn, he examined the food being fed the stock and, recalling a bit of knowledge he had picked up somewhere, made suggestions for a better feeding plan. As the days went by, he did any number of things to improve the farm, even going to town and bargaining for new implements, and finding better markets for Farmer Carver's produce. Some instinct seemed to guide him to better ways of doing everyday things.

Each night he slept in his mother's cabin. Since log cabins are sturdy and stand up under much abuse and neglect, even though this cabin had not been used for years, after he had swept and dusted it thoroughly, it made an ideal summer house. Air passed freely through the wide cracks and as he lay on his cot at night he could look up at the stars. Early mornings he went into the woods, rediscovering old delights. Again he brought back plants and mosses and set them in the yard. He visited his fish pond.

He had told them about Aunt Mariah and Uncle Andy and one evening he asked Farmer Carver if he might use the cart to drive over to Neosho and visit them. The farmer consented gladly, and early the next morning George once more turned his face in that direction. He remembered every foot of the road, recalling vividly that long and tedious trip on foot. Now it seemed so much shorter and the town much smaller. He drove rapidly, scourged by fear which he tried to thrust out of his mind. It grew as he turned down the narrow familiar street. Once before he had gone back to find a friend— What if—?

No sooner had he sighted the cabin than he could have shouted. There was Aunt Mariah—her arms buried in the frothy suds and there, his chair tilted back against the apple tree, was Uncle Andy. Nothing had changed.

It was a happy day for the three of them. George would not allow Aunt Mariah to stop her work to serve him. Instead, he helped her finish it. He had brought food stuffs in the cart and now he set about preparing a feast. While the food was simmering in pans he emptied her tubs, demonstrated how tall he was by spreading sheets along the line with ease. She protested. He was "company" and "all dressed up," but George only laughed.

They exclaimed over his cooking, marveling at the food. Later they sat out in the yard and talked. George told them all the things he'd done, where he had been. Almost timidly Uncle Andy brought the Bible and asked him to read. Scarcely glancing at the page he read the 23rd Psalm and then in the same voice he recited Bryant's "Thanatopsis." Aunt Mariah cried softly. It was very late when he drove back to Diamond Grove. He had followed the stars through the night and caught the "glory of the firmament."

As the summer began to wane the Carvers begged George to remain. But George shook his head.

"I cannot. I have work to do. It's lovely here, but I—" he looked down at his hands, spreading his long fingers, "I have so much to learn."

"What more do you want to know?" asked the farmer. "You read and write and spell, you're smart as a whip with figures, and you have seen much of the world."

"These things will be useful. But they are just the beginning. I must go to college," George told him.

"But, George," said Frau Carver, almost timidly. "Negroes don't go to college. What will you do with so much learning? There will be no place for you to work."

"Do not worry. *I* am going to college, and when I have read all the books and learned all that teachers can tell me, then God will open up His secrets to me. There will be work for me to do on His great earth. All things are His."

Frau Carver turned to her husband. "Let him alone, *mein Mann!* The boy is right. God does not make mistakes!"

He was preparing to leave. In a corner of the cabin still stood his mother's spinning wheel. He asked if he could take it with him and they gladly assented. For the remainder of his life he kept it in his room.

And so one morning they stood on the porch and waved good-bye, the big, red farmer who no longer appeared so great and towering, and his white-haired, sweet-faced wife. There were tears in her eyes, but she was proud of her little black boy—the sickly, puny, coughing baby over whom she had whispered, "Mary's child *must* live!"

He never saw them again.

Years later, as the boy, now a man, drove through the streets of Washington, he hoped they knew.

"Yes," thought Dr. George Washington Carver as the taxi took him to the Capitol building, "I am sure they see me now."

7. "GENTLEMEN, I GIVE YOU THE PEANUT!"

FOR THREE DAYS now the Ways and Means Committee of the United States Senate had been listening to reasons why they should or should not pass a certain tariff bill which had come up before the house. The bill had been introduced by Congressmen Hawley and Smoot and was designed to protect the producers of this country from infringement of their rights by putting a high tariff on the same products as they came into the country. Rice, for instance, could be raised in China for a few cents a bushel. In 1921 China was not at war and coolies worked for next to nothing. It cost so little to raise the rice that even after shipping it over here, it could sell for much less than the rice raised in our own country. Our growers did not want such competition.

The Congressman from South Dakota quite agreed—

about rice and wheat and corn. But, as the Congressman from Pennsylvania said, and not too softly, the hearings were becoming tedious. Before the Committee had come spokesmen for meat packers, poultry farmers, dairymen, manufacturers, date growers, walnut growers. All of them brought statistics which they presented in a highly efficient manner. Now, to cap the climax somebody from the Virginia-Carolina Cooperative Peanut Exchange was complaining because they could not sell their peanuts! This was carrying the matter too far. Peanuts! Monkey-food, boys called them. Fine to munch at a circus, but surely nobody was seriously thinking of including *peanuts* in a tariff bill!

The Congressman from Michigan got up and wandered out. Another man representing the New York Peanut Association was pointing out that "whereas the present tariff imposes duty of three-eighths of one cent per pound on unshelled peanuts and three-fourths of one cent on shelled peanuts it affords no protection to American producers. We are asking that—" The voice went on. Sheets were being rustled. Somebody dropped a book.

One of the officials of the United Peanut Growers Association groaned audibly and whispered to the man beside him, "It's no use, Bill. We're sunk!"

"Steady," whispered back the other man, "it's two-thirty. This room's so crowded, we can't see who's in the back. Maybe he's here."

The speaker had finished and the chairman fitted his glasses and peered at the sheet before him. "Thank you, Mr. Smith. Now," he looked closely, "Mr. Carver—is Mr. Carver in the room?"

The two officials held their breath. There was a move-ment near the door where several men were standing. No one had come forward, and the chairman said, "We'll go on. I guess Mr. Carver is not here. Will Mr.—"

"Pardon me, sir," a high, shrill voice was heard in the back of the room, "this case is heavy and awkward. It's difficult to get through."

Heads were turned and a way cleared in the aisle. Then the Congressmen saw the slender, slightly stooped Negro, in his green-black alpaca, carrying a large wooden case. Under his arm was the old golf cap. Having reached the front of the room, he eased the case to the floor, stuffed the cap in his pocket and stood waiting. The chairman stared at him.

"What—what—?"

"I am George Washington Carver."

"Oh—oh, yes. You've come to speak on the tariff."

Several gentlemen in the room could not help laughing. One man asked bluntly, "What do you know about the Hawley-Smoot bill?" There was laughter.

But the old man turned and with a twinkle in his eye said, "Not a thing. Do you?" When the laughter had died down he added, smiling, "I've come to talk about peanuts!"

The chairman had to rap for order. He said rather sternly, "Very well, Mr. Carver, will you please come to the stand? You have ten minutes."

They leaned forward to see as the unusual figure stepped up, opened his case and began talking.

"I've been asked by the United Peanut Growers Associ-ation to tell you something about the possibility of the peanut and its possible extension," he began. "I come from

Tuskegee, Alabama, where I am engaged in agricultural research work. I have given some attention to the peanut and can tell you that it is one of the very richest of all the products of the soil—rich in food value, rich in properties of its chemical constituents, and wonderfully rich in possibilities for utilization."

The Congressmen were leaning forward, their eyes eager. Now the Negro opened his case and was removing the contents: bottles of every size, description and color, little boxes, several small plaques.

"If I may have a little space to put these things down," he suggested. And the clerk quickly cleared the table for him.

"Thank you," said Mr. Carver. "Now I should like to exhibit them to you. I am going to just touch a few high places here and there, because in ten minutes you will tell me to stop. These are a few of the products which we have developed from the peanut." He held up a tube. "This is breakfast food containing peanut and sweet potato —twin brothers. It is wholesome, easily digested and delicious in flavor. A perfectly balanced diet with all the nutriments in it could be made from the sweet potato and peanut."

One of the Congressmen took the tube in his hand and examined it.

"Here is ice cream powder made from the peanut," continued Mr. Carver. "Simply mixed with water, it produces an unusually rich and delicious ice cream, not to be distinguished from ice cream made with pure cream." He held up several small bottles of different color. "In these bottles are dyes extracted from the skin of peanuts.

I have found thirty different dyes. They have been tested in the laboratory and found to hold their colors and to be harmless to the skin. Here is a substitute for quinine. We can hardly overestimate the medicinal properties of the peanut. They are many and varied. These are various kinds of food for live stock. You will find that cattle thrive on them and the increase in milk is pronounced."

He looked up at the wall clock and remarked.

"I see my time is about up. I should like to say that the soil and climate of the South is particularly suited to the cultivation of peanuts and that they could be produced in much greater quantities if a larger market for them were developed."

He stopped and began gathering up his bottles. The Congressmen looked at each other with amazement. Mr. Garner, from the back of the room, called out, "Mr. Chairman, all this is very interesting. I think his time should be extended."

"Very well, gentlemen," answered the chairman, "do you all agree?"

"Yes! Yes!" they answered in one voice.

"Will you continue, Mr. Carver," asked the chairman, smiling.

"I shall be happy to do so, sir."

From the front row Mr. Rainey asked, "Is the varied use of the peanut increasing?"

"Oh, yes," came the quick reply, "we are just beginning to know its value."

"In that case, is it not going to be such a valuable product that the more we have of them here the better we are off?"

"Gentlemen, I give you the peanut!"

"Well, now that depends. It depends upon the problems that these other gentlemen have brought before you," declared Mr. Carver, with a smile.

"Could we get too much of them—they being so valuable for stock food and everything else?" asked a man at the back of the room.

"Well, of course, we would have to have protection for them." There was laughter. "That is, we could not allow other countries to come in and take over our rights."

"I thought you said you didn't know anything about tariff," called out a voice.

"Well, I know it's what keeps the other fellow out of our business!" replied the old man. When the laughter had died down he went on, "I wish to say here in all sincerity that America produces better peanuts than any other part of the world, so far as I have been able to find out."

"Then," said Mr. Rainey, "we need not fear these inferior peanuts from abroad at all. They would not compete with our better peanuts."

"Well, you know that's like everything else. You know some people like oleomargarine just as well as they do butter. So sometimes you have to protect a good thing."

"The dairy people did not ask for a tax on oleomargarine," Mr. Oldfield spoke up, "but they did put a tax on butter."

"And," said Mr. Garner, "they did use the taxing power to put it out of business."

"Oh, yes, yes, sir. That is all the tariff means—to put the other fellow out." There was much laughter again.

The twinkling eyes turned to the chairman, "Maybe—maybe—I'd better stop!"

But the chairman leaned forward, wiping his eyes, "Go ahead, brother. Your time is unlimited."

"Well," picking up a small bottle, "here is milk from peanuts."

Mr. Oldfield laughed. "Don't you think we ought to put a tax on that peanut milk so as to keep it from competing with the dairy products?"

"No, sir. It is not going to affect the dairy product. It has a distinct value all its own."

"Why won't it replace the dairy product?" someone asked.

"We do not now have as much milk and butter as we need in the United States."

"How does it go in punch?" asked a teasing voice.

"Well," came the grave answer, "I'll show some punches."

"Attaboy!"

"Here is one with orange, here one with lemon, and this one with cherry!" Each time holding up a bottle with different colored liquids. "Here is instant coffee which already has in it cream and sugar, here is the preparation for making regular coffee. Here is buttermilk, Worchestershire sauce, pickles—all made from the peanut!"

There was a moment of breathless silence. Then someone asked, "Did you make all those products yourself?"

"Yes, sir, they are made in the research laboratory. That's what a research laboratory is for. The sweet potato products number one hundred and seven up to date."

Mr. Garner leaned forward, "What? I didn't catch that last statement."

"From sweet potatoes we have made ink, relishes, pomade, mucilage, to mention only a few things. But I must stick to peanuts." There was laughter. "Here are mock oysters which would fool most of you. I have developed recipes for mock meat dishes from peanuts. They are delicious. We are going to use less and less meat as science develops the products of nature."

"So, you're going to ruin the live stock business!" came a voice.

"Oh, no, but peanuts can be eaten when meat can't. Peanuts are the perfect food. They are always safe. God has given them to us for our use. He has revealed to me some of the wonders of this fruit of His earth. In the first chapter of Genesis we are told, 'Behold, I have given you every herb that bears seed upon the face of the earth, and every tree bearing seed. To you it shall be meat.' That's what He means about it—meat. There is everything there to strengthen, nourish and keep the body alive and healthy."

The chairman cut in here to ask, "Mr. Carver, where did you go to school?"

"The last school I attended was Agricultural College of Iowa. You doubtless remember Mr. Wilson, who served in the Cabinet here so long, Secretary James Wilson. He was my teacher for six years."

Several Congressmen nodded their heads. "What research laboratory do you work in now?" asked one.

"I am at Tuskegee Institute, Tuskegee, Alabama."

Mr. Carew rose, "You have rendered this committee a great service."

"I think," said Mr. Garner, "he is entitled to the thanks of the committee."

Every member stood up, clapping heartily.

"Did the Institute send you here or did you come of your own volition?"

"I was asked to come by the United Peanut Growers Association to talk about," he paused and his eyes twinkled again,—"peanuts!"

There was more warm, hearty laughter. One Congressman called out, "Come again soon, and bring the rest of your products with you."

The bottles had been carefully replaced in the case. The chairman leaned forward and said sincerely, "We want to compliment you, sir, on the way you have handled your subject."

Dr. Carver bowed with gracious dignity, presented his brief to the clerk and walked quietly from the room.

"Well, I'll be blowed!" The official of the United Peanut Growers Association wiped the perspiration from his brow.

"And you were going to tell him what to say!" commented his companion.

"Aw, shut up!" grinned the official.

The committee moved that the hearings were finished. Its members rose, adjourned to another room and voted to include the peanut in the Hawley-Smoot Tariff Bill.

In the late afternoon sunshine an insignificant black man paused one moment under the sleeping arch, then descended the Capitol steps.

It was over. Now, he could go back to his laboratory!

PART II

THE EARTH IS THE LORD'S

8. COLLEGE DEGREES

GEORGE HAD SAID he was going to college. The announcement sent out by Highland University offered him the fulfillment of his dreams. Highland was in Kansas, a small college, but, so the circular stated, prepared to train "gentlemen and ladies in all the letters and arts." Uncle Seymour noted that it was a Presbyterian school and heartily approved. George filled in the application blank carefully and mailed it with shaking fingers. In due time came the reply. He was accepted and with scholarship honors!

In after years, George Washington Carver, the man, shied away from the memory of what happened then. He arrived at Highland University with such surging anticipation and was directed to the office of the President. It was the most impressive room he had ever seen, with

93

bookcases along the walls and a polished desk. But the face of the man behind the desk became quickly blurred, after the verdict that blasted young George's hopes.

"Sorry, there must have been some mistake!"

The words were cold and very definite.

"But—but—this—this—is the day. You—your letter—"

George stopped and with a mighty effort of will sought to control the shameful stammering which even yet shattered his speech under emotional strain. They were not going to admit him. They were going to turn him away. But that couldn't be. He had a scholarship. His letter had said "Report September 15th." He laid the open sheet on the desk.

The President of the college stared down at his own signature. His thoughts were whirling! How could he have ever suspected? The application received that summer had shown an unusual high school record from Minneapolis High School, one of the best in the state. But, good heavens—a Negro! The brown hands gripping his desk were rusty and work-worn, the sleeves of the coat threadbare—a thin, gangling country fellow! The President's eyes shifted uneasily from the burning intensity of that penetrating gaze. And because of his discomfort, his voice was almost harsh.

"You did not say in your application that you were—colored."

"I answered all the questions. I—I—did not—think—" the boy's voice cracked.

The President cleared his throat. "I do regret this, young man, but there is no provision here for Negro students. So far as I know, you are the first to apply."

George turned away and started for the door. There was no more to say. But the man stopped him.

"Tell me, why should you want to go to college? You've finished high school. For one of your race, that is very good indeed. What would you do with a college education? There are no openings. Frankly, it seems to me you would be wasting your time—and ours."

George had reached the door. Now he turned and with his hand on the knob, said simply, "Time belongs to God. I am going to college because there is work for me to do and I must be ready."

He closed the door softly behind him. The man at the desk sat motionless, then he made a sudden movement to rise, stretched out his hand as if to call. His lips formed the words.

After a moment, however, he fell back into his seat, shaking his head, "I couldn't," he murmured, "it would never do—a Negro!"

George walked away, at first blindly, but as the warm September sun enveloped him, the muscles of his throat relaxed, the pain in his chest lessened and he saw the loveliness of Indian summer all around him. The streets of the little town fanned out from the college showing rows of frame houses and crude weather-beaten shops. On every side were signs of student life—bookshops and boarding houses; solemn, bearded young men, their pants tucked inside boots in the approved fashion, some of them even wearing collars. These obviously were city boys with "store-bought" clothes.

All of them seemed preoccupied and very busy. George wondered about them, where they had come from, where they would live. He sighed. Well, one thing was certain. He could not go back. He thought of the weeks he had waited anxiously for a reply to his college application. And when it had come—and with that tuition scholarship! He had told everybody. They had rejoiced with him. He had gone by to see Big Nat and Nat had boomed out the news to his customers. Then George had left his job at the restaurant and had spent his money in preparation for college. Aunt Lucy had given him a bag into which he had packed his few belongings, leaving only his mother's spinning wheel with her until he was settled. Now, here he was!

He had no money. He must find work. In his musing he had reached the edge of the town. Ahead, lay the country road. It was harvest time. Hands would be needed, so he walked on. That night he slept and slept well in a hay loft upon a fragrant bed of new mown hay. Already, he had a job and, sooner or later, he would go to college.

Time belonged to God.

This was in 1886. As he worked in the fields, George heard talk of "homesteading." He learned that the government was giving away land in western Kansas to anyone who would live on it. This seemed pretty wonderful to George and he took in every detail on filing a claim. He made up his mind that if he could not go to school, he could set about the business of growing things—and on his own land.

So George "trekked" westward and near the town of Beeler, in Ness County, took up one hundred and sixty acres of good Kansas soil and on it built himself a tiny house. This was not the time of year for planting and since he had no live stock and knew nothing about preparing soil for crops, George hired out at a nearby ranch that first winter.

In the spring George returned to his own land and set hard to work. His hut stood in the middle of the rolling, desert prairie. It burst in bloom before his startled eyes. In all that vast expanse of sky and riotous earth, the boy became a man. He shook off hurts and disappointments which had seemed so great. He took on height and stature. His mind and soul reached up and stretched forth wings which, in the years to come, no scorn or ridicule could ever clip.

His land was poor, best fit for grazing. And at first George did not mind. He wandered over the desert, finding strange plants, drawing pictures of them and absorbing the rich colors of a prairie sunset. Once he nearly lost his life in a fierce Kansas blizzard.

He was happy, but the time came at length when George knew he must leave. School still awaited him— somewhere. He had not yet read "all the books." He knew that he had drawn strength from the land. But even though the homestead period was not fulfilled and the land not yet his, he felt that he must now go on. So he packed his things with no regrets and crossed the border into Iowa.

Winterset might have taken its name from a bleakness of weather-beaten houses set down in the midst of stubble prairie. Like other Iowa towns, it had been in the path of the plague which had swept over the state. People still spoke with horror of grasshoppers. Farmers could never be sure they would not come again. Each harvest was watched with anxiety. For in 1873, the grasshoppers had come in swarms, "obscuring the sun" in their flight. They came "with a roaring noise like the sound of a waterfall." After they had passed it was "as though the country had been swept by a prairie fire." Again, in 1874 and in '76 they had come. Many farmers had then sold out or simply moved away from their lands. Towns were left almost like deserted villages.

The farmers who had remained faced frightful odds. But for years now they had been left in peace and the cottonwood and soft maple trees were untouched. But there were still no flower gardens or grass before the houses. And life was hard. Families arose at five o'clock, and time was wasted that was not spent in work. Living was cheap. Two or three dollars would buy a winter's supply of potatoes for a family and potatoes were filling. Farmers sold corn for fifteen cents a bushel and their wives brought eggs to town and sold them for eight and nine cents a dozen.

George got a job cooking at the Schultz Hotel in Winterset. He slept on a cot in the hotel shed, his meals were included in his wages, so he could save most of what he earned. Ease and comforts were almost considered sinful in Winterset. Life habits were crystallizing within George's character. The hard way was always to seem the best way to him and waste a sin which could not be forgiven.

He was a young man now, no longer undersized and puny. Within the past six months he had shot up to six feet. He carried himself well and was growing a mustache. He had not overcome his shyness with people, however, and he resolved he must no longer avoid them. People also were God's creatures. Although, he thought ruefully, he still preferred the "little people" of the woods!

Remembering how the Martins had sent him to church, he resolved again to follow their advice. There were only two colored families in Winterset and therefore no colored church. On his next Sunday "off," George, after carefully waxing his boots and brushing his "best" coat, donned a shirt which he himself had laundered and appeared at the large whitewashed church near the center of town.

He slipped in quietly and took a seat in the rear. Service had not yet begun so he had time to look about, observing the group seated together on an elevated platform near the organ and examining the hymn book on the pew beside him. When the opening hymn was announced, he turned to it eagerly. He liked to sing and being accustomed to congregational singing he found the place and waited attentively while the organ sounded the short prelude. "A Mighty Fortress is our God"—yes, Frau Carver used to hum the tune as she went about her work and even the farmer's occasional loud voice boomed forth words which George now knew were German, but certainly the song was the same.

So he joined in heartily with the opening line and was well along in the hymn before he realized that heads in the congregation were turning in his direction. Then he noted to his dismay that those around him were not singing, only the people on the platform. He stopped, embarrassed.

But a white-haired little lady sitting behind him leaned

over and, tapping him lightly with her fan, whispered, "Sing right out, young man. God gave you that voice."

He smiled at her, but not until the audience rose to its feet to sing the Doxology was his voice heard again. Then once more it rose clear and sweet and young, and after the benediction people turned to him with out-stretched hands and welcomed the tall dark stranger.

The following Sunday, he went to church again and the pastor took his name and repeated it to himself as he wrote it down. He found out where George was working and during the following week managed to throw several odd jobs his way. George became a regular attendant at the church. He understood now that most of the singing was done by the choir, and he enjoyed listening to them. But even more he enjoyed lifting his own voice in the final hymn.

One day, after the rush of the noon meal was over, one of the "front" hotel boys stuck his head in the kitchen, motioned to George and said, "Gen'leman to see you inside!"

He whisked away so quickly that George, surprised, did not have time to question him. Before he could remove the greasy apron and wash his hands, the door swung back admitting a heavy-set pleasant man whose face was vaguely familiar.

"Ah, here you are, George. Don't stop. Pastor told me you worked here and I thought I'd stop by and see you a minute. My name is Millholland."

George remembered him then as one of the men who had shaken hands with him at church. He smiled.

"This—this kitchen isn't any place for visitors," he began apologetically.

"Don't mind that. My wife and I know you must be pretty lonely here, and we'd like to have you come over to our house some evening."

"Oh!" George was completely taken unawares by the invitation. He did not know what to say.

"My wife leads the choir at church. She heard you singing. You see, she's a musician, trained abroad, and knows a good voice when she hears one."

"You mean that I—" George stopped. The idea was too much.

"Why, yes, she says you've a good, powerful voice."

"I couldn't even talk a few years ago!"

"Is that so!" Mr. Millholland's face expressed his amazement. "Well, that makes it even more remarkable. When can you come?"

An evening was decided upon and after giving him directions as to finding the house, Mr. Millholland went away, leaving a smiling young man. In those days only the very rich traveled to Europe, so George concluded that the Millhollands must be very fine indeed. Mrs. Millholland, a trained musician, had noticed his voice! And now they were inviting him to their home. Such amazing good fortune!

At last the important evening actually arrived. For perhaps the first time in his life, George considered his wardrobe wholly inadequate. He carefully mended a break in his boots and then rubbed them well with lard and stove blacking. His clothes were clean, for he had washed and ironed even his pants and coat. He scrubbed his hands until the skin smarted.

But as he set out for the house, he was far from satisfied. It was early spring. The last snows had just disappeared and the ground was still muddy. Just as he took the last turn beyond the maple tree, he saw almost hidden behind a rock wall a little blue flower. It stood alone, valiantly lifting itself out of the mud. George stopped.

Then he whispered, "You're here, waiting for me, aren't you, little flower. Oh, you lovely little blue flower!"

Stooping, he plucked it gently, being careful to break the stem evenly at the base. He cupped it in his hand, looking deeply into its heart. Then, sticking it into the buttonhole of his coat he went forward. Now, he felt "arrayed like unto the lilies of the valley."

Mr. Millholland himself admitted George and ushered him into the front room. Leaving the visitor alone, he went back to call his wife. George looked about him, his first impression one of disappointment. The room seemed so bare. "Parlors" at that time were usually jammed with sofas and chairs of every description, atrocious pictures crowded the walls, wax flowers in glass cases were numerous and huge Bibles, albums and all kinds of adornments were plentiful. But here was a sense of spacious emptiness.

And then he saw it! Close beside the wide window, its flat, shining surface reflecting the last rays of a dying sun stood a piano! George knew what it was from pictures he had seen at school. It stood upon slender, delicate legs. He tip-toed around so that he could examine the white and black key board. His long, delicate fingers spread out over the keys. One sounded faintly and he started back, but a pleasant, smiling voice said softly,

"Don't move. Your hands match your voice. You are an artist."

He turned then and faced Mrs. Millholland. Yes, he had listened to her singing in the choir and had watched her face beneath the coiled white hair. It was true, what he had thought. She was not like the others. Something was rare and different. At the moment he could hear only the music in her voice.

"Won't you sit down? I'd like to play for you."

Her white fingers caressed the keys and then she began to play. With the true artist's instinct she chose "Les Preludes." She knew how well they would speak to this lanky black youth with his long slender hands and blazing, deep-set eyes. She played and brought back memories of her youth in Paris, of boulevards and gardens with their fountains playing in the moonlight, of Victor Hugo, Dumas and Chopin, coughing his heart out as he poured his music at the feet of George Sands. She played, and as she played the room faded for the black boy and he was back in the woods with all his "little people." He lay on his stomach and listened to the murmuring of the brook, pressed his face again in dew-drenched violets and felt the cool clear water slipping through his fingers. She played and slowly the frustration of all her wasted years pressed down. The long, long years of dreams going one by one. And suddenly the room rang with the cry of mighty Beethoven—Beethoven, beating his wings against the sky, climbing the mountain of his greatness. George could no longer breathe. He heard the call—clear—so clear

—coming from mountain tops—"The earth! The earth is the Lord's! Lift up your eyes to the hills." Again he saw them! Again, he stood beside Hermann Jaegar—The pain! The terrible pain was engulfing him! He cried out! And covered his face with his hands. His body shook, while tears squeezed through his fingers. He had lost his hills.

The room was very still and then Mrs. Millholland was saying, her voice filled with contrition, "My friend, oh, my young friend, forgive me!"

George only shook his head. For a while he could not speak. Finally he managed to whisper,

"It—it—was—so—beautiful! I—I—" he pressed his lips tightly.

"I do understand. I should have known better."

She smiled at him and then George understood that once more he had met one of those who truly see. Some secret recess in his heart opened and a glow of happiness filled his being.

Before he left that evening, he had told Mr. and Mrs. Millholland all about the bitter disappointment of his refusal at Highland University, of the Carvers and his early days on the farm, of his travels searching for knowledge, and now of his determination to go to college. Never had he talked so freely to anyone and never could he have had a more attentive audience. He promised to return soon, to bring some of his paintings. They promised to begin inquiries at once for a college which would accept him and as he rose to go Mrs. Millholland said,

"Time is always granted us for something, if we will but use it. While you are here, you shall be my music pupil."

With simple dignity George accepted her offer and made one in return, "And I will make you a garden. I'll find grasses and flowers and you shall have the loveliest of gardens."

It was a bargain. And that spring was one of the happiest he was to remember. Every hour George could spare away from the hotel he spent digging, planting and tending the garden which slowly took form in the Millholland yard, or he practiced at the piano. His flowers bloomed, and each week his fingers became more apt with the keys. He learned rapidly, as Mrs. Millholland had predicted he would. One of his water colors now hung on her wall. Visitors admired it and could scarcely believe that it had been painted by the tall dark boy who had joined their church choir.

Summer came quickly. One evening, George appeared later than usual and went immediately to the shed behind the Millhollands' house. He was busy at his bench when from the porch he heard Mrs. Millholland calling,

"George, George! Come here. We have a visitor!"

George left his work reluctantly. But the young man seated astride the porch railing was anything but formidable. George later learned that it was a nervous trick of running his fingers through his thick red hair that kept it standing on ends. It gave his face a certain impishness and the little student beard did not conceal the freckles. He extended his hand while Mrs. Millholland announced,

"George, this is my nephew, Dan Brown."

"And you're George Washington Carver. Well, you may not have heard of me, but I've certainly been told a lot about you."

"Not everything, I hope." George instantly responded to the cordial friendliness in tone and manner.

"Sit down, George. Dan brings us good news."

George sank down on the top step. Mrs. Millholland's eyes were beaming and his mind leaped forward towards dazzling possibilities. Dan Brown was taking in the well-shaped head and keen, eager face. Something of anticipation stirred within him, also. Here was a student! He leaned forward.

"They tell me you want to go to college. Well, Simpson's your school!" he said.

"Simpson?" George shook his head. "I've never heard of it. Where is it? And do you think they'll take me?"

"One question at a time, me lad. Simpson is a Methodist school at Indianola, Iowa. Old Bishop Mathew Simpson, an Abolitionist and life-long friend of Abraham Lincoln, left all his land and fortune for its establishment. They'll receive you gladly."

George looked at him with shining eyes.

"Dan's a student there himself," said Mrs. Millholland, "and he says he'll write them at once."

"You will?" George gasped.

"Sure. You'll have until fall to get yourself together. The tuition isn't too much, and Indianola is a fair-sized town where you can find work."

"Are there any colored students there?" was George's next question.

"No, I've never heard of any," Dan thought a moment, then went on, "but you'll see that will make no difference. Bishop Simpson would turn over in his grave if they went against the principles which he fought for all his life."

"Rising up and haunting them would be more effective," Mrs. Millholland remarked laughingly.

George could no longer remain seated. He had to stand up and fill his lungs with air. At last, the way was opening.

"And they say there's a very good Art Department. You see," Mrs. Millholland was explaining to Dan, "I think George ought to major in Art. He can do so many things, but you know those two paintings I showed you are unusual. He could even major in music," she added.

Dan was regarding George. He answered slowly, "Yes, the paintings are—unusual, but—" he stopped.

"But *what?*" Mrs. Millholland insisted, quick to defend her pupil.

"Well, I don't know. I may be wrong, but, Aunt Nell, when I compare this yard with the one I saw here last summer, it seems to me George's greatest gift lies with growing living things, rather than in mere reproductions on canvas—or even, with deep apologies to all present artists, on the piano." He bowed with mock gravity.

George recognized the compliment and together they laughed. Mrs. Millholland was not so sure. She left them together, and they went out into the gardens—the tall, serious young white man with his understanding and appreciation and the tall, eager-eyed young black man to whom the hour meant more than food and drink. It passed all too quickly, and George hurried back to work.

Now each day had new meaning. He was going to Simpson College! He decided not to write in advance. But a couple of days before the opening, he left Indianola and within an amazingly short time had registered and was enrolled as a student at Simpson. The fact that traveling expenses and tuition had taken all his money in no way dampened his soaring spirits. Sleeping quarters were furnished at the college. His immediate problem was food. Out of his remaining thirteen cents he bought five cents' worth of cornmeal and five cents' worth of suet. Actually, because food was cheap, he had two large packages.

The mixture which he himself prepared served to feed him that first week. By the end of this time he had done enough odd jobs to have acquired some capital. He bought a washtub and board, was granted the use of a woodshed, and here he again went into business for himself. His friend, Dan Brown, drummed up trade, and soon the old woodshed became the Mecca for the college boys. George not only washed and ironed their shirts, finishing them with polished perfection, but he mended and sewed on buttons, darned socks, patched and turned pants. While he worked, the boys sat around during the long evenings after classes, exchanging ideas and jokes, quizzing each other for exams.

And sometimes George told stories in a droll, witty manner which captivated and delighted his listeners.

He not only became popular, but was spoken of as a genius. Twenty-seven of the oil paintings now hanging in the Carver Art Collection were done during the next three years under the guidance of Miss Etta M. Budd, director of the School of Art, Simpson College. His work was held up before the other students. Acclaimed as the artist, he continued his music and played on student recitals. He also sang with the chorus.

At first all this seemed too wonderful for any questioning. But during his second year George became disturbed by vague doubts. They said of his paintings, "You can scarcely tell Carver's plants and flowers from those that grow in our gardens!"

That was true. But these painted plants and flowers could not speak to George. He missed something.

His second year he spent more time in the laboratory. And soon his teachers began to say frankly, "We don't have the facilities for you here, George."

So it was that George Washington Carver came face to face with the greatest decision of his life.

His art teacher held before him visions of Paris, of the famous art schools of Europe, of recognition and perhaps fame. She said he would succeed. He loved his painting.

And yet—

As he studied his long fingers which now wielded the brush so skillfully, he remembered that deep, full voice and the thrill which the little boy had felt warmed him again,

"You have the hand of a gardener—your touch will bring life!"

To *bring* life—not merely copy life!

And so, in 1891 George Washington Carver left Simpson College and entered Iowa State College at Ames, a great institution already well known for its excellent departments in botany and agricultural chemistry.

He was almost twenty-seven years old, tall and straight and now very sure of himself. With his excellent recommendations from Simpson, he encountered no difficulties in entering Ames. He had not only the money for his tuition, but also enough for the regular dormitory fees.

But here was trouble. The authorities would not allow a Negro student to live in the dormitory.

At that time James Wilson, later to be Secretary Wilson, a member of the United States Cabinet, was director of the United States Experimental Station at Iowa State College. Hearing of the plight of this new student, he sought him out and with no formality said,

"Deuce take their rules! George, you can move right into my office!"

They shifted the office furniture around and carried in a cot. The cot stuck in the doorway. Only by turning and pulling could they get it through the narrow opening. Then George ruefully surveyed the ragged mark left on the woodwork.

"I can stain the whole doorway so it won't show," he offered.

The professor shrugged his shoulders. "There's lots of scarred woodwork and battered furniture around here. Needn't get fussy about one little scratch."

George looked about the crowded room. It was shabby and worn. His face lit with a smile. He could repay this kind man for his hospitality.

"Is there a paint shop on the campus?" he asked, ready to start at once.

"Paint shop? I don't know. This isn't an art school, you know." Mr. Wilson was already gathering up his notebooks. He was a very busy man.

"But every school should have a paint shop, a place where students can learn how to use the wonderful colors God has placed all around us. Some day I'll have such a

The cot stuck in the doorway.

place and students will come to me because they *want* to come." George was enthusiastic.

Mr. Wilson looked closely into the bright eyes burning so intensely in that dark face. Anticipation stirred within him. Here was no ordinary student! They were to become life-long friends, but James Wilson never ceased to marvel.

George set out looking for a paint shop. As he walked across the campus he heard music—a band playing. He could not resist and turned his steps in the direction of the music. In a few minutes he came out on a wide parade ground and there, in close formation, heads up, bayonets flashing in the afternoon sunshine marched—soldiers! It was an impressive sight and George caught his breath sharply.

"Oh, dear! I'll not be able to keep up!"

The plaintive voice at his elbow startled George. He looked around and blinked! Never had he seen such a fat young man. The round, moonlike face glistened with moist beads; the small eyes were intent upon the marching ranks but the blue-coated figures stepping so briskly to the martial music seemed to fill him with apprehension. George could not understand.

"Keep up? What do you mean?" Then a startling explanation dawned. Eyes on the rotund form, George almost laughed aloud. "Are *you* going to be a soldier?"

"Rolly," as his friends called him, turned his head. Now, it was his turn to stare.

"You must be the—" he stopped, hesitating to use the word which he had heard applied to people of this tall young man's color. He had heard of this new student's unexpected appearance on the campus. All the fellows had. He had heard them talking about it, speculating on what he would be like and whether or not he would stay. Rolly had come from a small town in Minnesota. He had never before seen a Negro. Now, he looked hard at George. He was disappointed. Clearly, this was no "heathen," much less a "cannibal." He didn't resemble any of the pictures he had seen.

George, fully aware of some of these thoughts, smiled and said, "I'm a new student, came only yesterday. Have you been here long?"

Rolly sighed. His mind reverted to his immediate worries.

"No. This is my first year, too. But don't you know all male students here have to join the National Guards?"

"National Guards?"

"Yes—them!" Rolly pointed in the direction of the disappearing soldiers.

George looked, but it was evident that he was puzzled.

"They," patiently explained the youth in a rather harassed tone, "are the advanced students in the National Guards. But all of us have to take it. It's called 'Military Tactics' in the catalogue and it means hours and hours of regular army training. The very thought makes me sick!" This was a long speech for Rolly and he relapsed into gloomy silence.

But George was interested.

"You mean—" his voice showed excitement.

"Yes, and when we graduate, we'll be regular army officers—lieutenants and captains—in Reserve," Rolly added in a dry, hollow tone.

They had turned and were walking back towards the

road. George asked no more questions. He was thinking. His concentration caused Rolly to emerge from his worried fretting. He began to wonder. Now, how could this dark student become an army officer? Had anybody ever heard of a Negro officer in the United States Army? *He* certainly never had. Was that what was bothering the young man now? His interest quickened and he glanced up at George's face, observing the fine profile and high forehead.

"He's probably very smart," thought Rolly. "He must be very smart—to be here." He decided he wanted to know something about him. For the moment he forgot himself and his problems.

George did not find the paint that afternoon. Rolly shared in his disappointment and the next morning the two of them went into town. George returned with everything he needed. Rolly had spent his allowance recklessly. He had never been so excited. George had opened an entirely new world of interest for him. The cost of a few paints and brushes was a small price to pay for so much.

Instead of sleeping on the cot that night, George painted and talked, his new friend following every stroke of the brush and every word with mounting interest. The spoiled, rich, fat boy had been very lonely. He had never been able to keep up with other boys. He always imagined that behind his back they were laughing at him. Anything unknown terrified him. In George he had found someone who had no fears at all! Rolly was amazed. George didn't seem to know that being black was a terrible handicap, that it took money to do things, that being alone in the world was—was— Well, he, Rolly, couldn't imagine anything worse. It would seem that George planned to go right on ahead, anyhow. Rolly gazed at him with something akin to awe!

And so it happened that the following Friday afternoon when all new students were to report for Military Tactics, Rolly waited until he saw George hurrying from the greenhouse and joined him.

With George he was not afraid.

It was the young Captain in charge who suffered a bad case of nerves. If George was unaware of his startled discomfort, Rolly, standing close by the dark youth's side, was not. He chuckled to himself and the last vestige of his own nervousness vanished. The Captain called the roll. He checked the name "George Washington Carver" when he observed who answered that name. But he was thinking rapidly. What was he to do? What could he do? There was no precedent. This was the first Negro to have enrolled in Iowa State College. As a regularly enrolled student, he was supposed to be placed in the cadet training course. After feverish speculation, made under the intent eyes of the staring fat boy, the Captain shrugged his shoulders. Let the higher-ups worry! And so George became a cadet in the Officers Reserve.

And now George began his work in earnest.

College students were older in those days and so while there was not so much difference between his age and that of the other students, he had already formed those habits which caused him to stand out. Long before the other students were up, he was down in the greenhouse or out in the woods. His keen eye saw everything. He knew from nature much they had to get from books and so by leaps and bounds he surpassed them.

George waited table in one of the halls, he became Mr. Wilson's right-hand man, he worked literally day and night. His one relaxation was found on the parade ground.

The other young men soon found that George could "take it." Quiet and reserved as he went about greenhouse or in classes, George became a ruling conqueror when he donned his uniform. He loved to march behind the brass band; the sight of the Stars and Stripes unfurling in the breeze stiffened his neck and sent a thrill of pride down his spine. Following the lead of his friend, Rolly gained confidence in himself and lost several pounds! He did not advance up through the ranks as rapidly as did George, but no faint shadow of envy touched him because of that. George continued to study his manual, memorizing rules, advancing until at the end of the first year, old General James Rush Lincoln barked his name in a loud, harsh voice and commissioned him Lieutenant.

The summer passed quickly. Somebody had to remain as caretaker for the greenhouse. Mr. Wilson was delighted when George asked for the job. He made one trip for a short visit with the Millhollands in Winterset, where his friends rejoiced in his progress and pressed him for every detail of his work.

Rolly did not return to Iowa State next fall. His parents had decided to send him to a more exclusive school in the east. From here he wrote George a long letter in which he urged George to come east for the Christmas holiday. Naturally, he offered to pay all expenses. George smiled warmly at the generous, but naive offer. He wrote thanking him, but explained how impossible it was for him to leave the greenhouse. He did miss Rolly.

Now he literally buried himself in his work. But one small boy singled him out. Several miles from the college campus on the outskirts of Ames was a vast tract of land still partially under water. The mud was overgrown with rank grasses and rushes. It was one of the few remaining sloughs, which at one time rendered useless much of the land in that section. This tract fascinated George. He had tested the soil and found it rich. He had already recommended to Mr. Wilson a method for draining away the water. For not only was the land going to waste, but in summer such places were breeding grounds for millions of mosquitoes and other poisonous insects. There were treacherous suck holes, and at certain spots the muddy waters were said to be bottomless. All together, it was a most dangerous place for a small boy to play.

One afternoon, as George with his bag, net and magnifying glass was starting back from the slough, he spied a boy, barefoot, pushing his way through the rushes. He was stepping from one projecting heap of mud to another.

"Hey!" George called quickly, "Come back here! Don't—"

Just then the boy slipped and fell.

It took only a moment to pull out the little fellow. He was not hurt, nor even badly frightened, but was certainly a sorry sight.

"Don't you know better than to go out there!" the young man cautioned. "You might have been sucked into the mud and drowned."

"Can't drown in mud!" retorted the boy, grinning.

"Well, you can smother in mud!"

"You said 'drown'!" The boy was regarding George gravely. "Now," he announced, "I've seen you with that bag. What are you doing?"

"Gathering specimens for the college."

George had wiped the boy off as well as he could. But he had not finished with his lecture. "And why should you want to go about breaking down little people's houses?" he went on, sternly.

The boy opened his eyes wide. "Houses?" he asked, puzzled.

Then George explained how the muskrats built their houses in the mud and he showed his audience of one how the projections gave the slough the appearance of a submerged village.

"Oh! I was mashing the roofs!" said the boy, appalled by the discovery.

"You certainly were!"

Tears filled the boy's eyes. Then George caught a large butterfly and spreading its wings, told the boy how it had come out of the mud. But when the boy wanted to keep it, George let the butterfly go and explained why. They talked for a long time and, as the sun was setting, walked across the campus.

"Do you come here every day?" the boy was curious.

"Not every day, but often."

"Could I come with you?"

"What will your mamma say? Just look at you now."

"When I tell her I fell in the mud—she'll be sorry. I'm

six, you know, and quite big enough to know better," the boy declared.

"What's your name?" George asked.

"Henry—Henry Wallace. What's yours?"

"Henry Wallace? Why you must be Mr. Wallace's son. He's one of my professors!" George was smiling.

"Oh, are you learning about cows, too?" the boy was not too impressed.

George laughed. "Your father is the teacher of dairying, it's true, but he knows a lot of other things, besides. And what's wrong with cows?"

"Nothing, I guess. Only, I don't like them. You didn't tell me your name."

George told him and they parted friends that day.

The following Saturday Henry appeared on the campus early in the morning. He found George in the greenhouse.

"Hello!" He hesitated, not certain of his welcome. Then, he held out a paper and said winsomely, "My grandpa writes about plants. Look!"

George smiled and took the paper. Aloud he read, "*Wallace's Farmer!* So, this is your grandfather's paper?"

"Yep," said the boy. "He lives in Des Moines. That's a big city. I've been there."

"You don't say," commented George politely.

"Are you going to the woods today?" The question was casual.

"Um-um," the answer was noncommittal. Then, "Is your mamma at home?" The boy nodded. "I think we'd better stop by and consult her."

And the young man and boy strolled away together.

Years later Henry Wallace said of this friendship, "That boy, who was myself, became a devoted follower and companion of the tall scientist, tagging him about as he cared for his flowers, and made long forays into the woods, bringing back what to the little boy appeared to be discoveries from fairyland."

When Vice-President Wallace was Secretary of Agriculture, he visited Tuskegee Institute and there addressing the students said, "Dr. Carver gave me credit for seeing differences in plants and grasses that I am sure I did not see. But it was the faith and charity that he extended to me as a small boy that did stir something within me."

One group of students George could not avoid, and later he did not try. One evening as he was going along the hall he heard someone groaning as if in great pain. He opened a door. A young man, half propped in bed, was twisting with agony. Instantly, George was beside him.

"What is it—what can I do?"

Between gasps the boy explained that he was a football player and had badly wrenched or perhaps broken his leg. George helped him to lie on his stomach and began gently to rub the leg from ankle to thigh. In a few minutes the boy was still. George continued the rubbing until he had fallen asleep. When the young man awoke, he found to his amazement that the pain had utterly gone. At practice next afternoon he told the entire team and within the next few days George found himself designated as the official "rubber." The boys declared his hands held magic, that he simply rubbed away pains and aches. In the spring during track meets, he was kept busy working over runners and high jumpers. Once he complained that the oil used was too heavy and did not spread well. The coach told him it was the best they could buy.

George held up the bottle a moment, looking through it and remarked thoughtfully, "I'm going to make a better rubbing oil!"

Several years later, he did—from peanuts!

In 1894 George Washington Carver received his Bachelor's Degree in Science from Iowa State College. By that time this momentous event was but a stepping-stone to him. Four of his paintings had been selected to hang in the Art Exhibit at the World's Columbian Exposition in 1893. He was hailed as one of Iowa's outstanding scholars. He had been commissioned Captain in the National Guards —perhaps the first Negro to hold this commission in the United States Officers Reserve.

As he walked upon the platform to receive his diploma he wore a wing collar and a black suit chosen more for its ironlike durability than for its cut. But he carried himself well. And the assembled students and their parents and friends applauded soundly.

Up to the moment of this graduation George had been so absorbed in his work that he had not thought beyond that day. As he took his diploma, the thought struck him:

"What am I going to do?"

It seemed a long time ago since he had been told there would be no place for him even should he succeed in getting a college education. Many friends came forward to congratulate him. Faculty and student body were proud of him, but that evening he walked across the campus and was very lonely. People had been kind, so kind—and yet—

He climbed the steps to his room on the top floor of one of the buildings. There in one corner stood his mother's spinning wheel. Softly he closed the door behind him and crossing the floor, fell on his knees beside it.

The child in him cried out to this mother from whom he had been so cruelly separated. Not to know where they had taken her, not to know some spot he might visit and pay her tribute—not to know—not to know! In this moment of his first complete triumph, he wanted his mother.

Darkness closed about the room and still he did not move. Gradually upon his consciousness came the sound of his name being called from below—

"George! George! Are you there?"

There were footsteps and then a quick knock on the door.

"Are you asleep, George?" The door opened admitting Professor Wilson. He stopped, sensing rather than actually seeing George in the corner.

"George, what are you doing up here in the dark all alone? Why—" And then he understood. His voice changed.

"My boy, we're waiting dinner for you at home. My wife sent me."

George had moved out to the table, and was fumbling with the oil lamp.

"You know," added Wilson, "you're a member of the faculty now!"

The lamp chimney slipped from George's shaking hand and crashed on the floor.

Mr. Wilson's voice was shaking, but he laughed. "Never mind that. Come! We can find our way down the stairs without a light. Some quarters you have up here—since you moved out of my office." He was trying to sound casual.

But George did not move. "You said—you said—"

"Yes, you were appointed this afternoon. Going to teach botany and have charge of the greenhouses. Come along and let's celebrate. T'intion, Captain Carver! Right face!"

He slipped his arm through George's and guided him toward the door.

To teach at Iowa State College! A member of the faculty—he—George Washington Carver! Surely, he had climbed the heights! What college graduate, white or black, could ask for more? And still horizons lay beyond. The Earth, God's Earth, was his—yet to discover!

9. "COME DOWN AND HELP US!"

IT WAS ALMOST two years later, and many miles from Iowa State College campus, far south in Alabama, that a big man, whom George had never seen, stood looking out a window.

Not that he could see very clearly. The pane was blurred with sheets of running water. It was raining. Not a gentle, soothing patter of pleasant showers, but torrents that soaked the earth and cut deep crevices in thick, red clay. It tore the young fruit from trees, beat down cornstalks and rotted cotton before it could be picked and pressed in bales.

The big man at the window sighed. Between this building and the next, a gully cut through the grounds. In dry weather students climbed it, but now a rushing stream threatened to overflow all the smooth, muddy surface, an ugly, yawning scar. There was no beauty in the bare, gaunt buildings under the leaden, gray sky. Everywhere, as far as he could see from the window, was ugliness! The man sighed again. He was trying to lead his people upward from slavery to independence and manhood, and this was the best he could offer.

The inability to read and write was common among those who grew up in Alabama after the War between the States. At that time thousands of children, white and black, in this state as well as throughout the South, had never seen inside a school. The few schools that existed were operated only when the children were not needed in the fields. Then churches and charitable institutions all over the country began to concern themselves about these children. Between 1880 and 1890 more than one hundred private and denominational schools were chartered. Among them was "Tuskegee Normal and Industrial Institute for Negroes." Lewis Adams, a former slave, was largely responsible for gaining the financial support of southern and northern white people for it. In 1881, General Armstrong sent the most promising graduate from Hampton Institute in Virginia to head this new school in the deep south. His name was Booker T. Washington.

Mr. Washington had found only a leaky old church and thirty students, some of them well past middle age, who wanted to learn their ABC's. He had taught them to read and write, to figure a little; he had gone out and raised money; had showed his students how to make brick, and they had constructed this first brick building. It was a good building. He knew that.

With this start, the students turned to and helped him. They had continued to make bricks from Alabama clay, this time to sell. Then many more students had come. Additional buildings went up. Mr. Washington made many speeches, carrying word of the school far and wide and winning support for it. Harvard University had conferred a degree upon him.

And yet, today, after fifteen years of unceasing labor, Booker T. Washington was discouraged.

So little had been accomplished. He had told his people to "let down your buckets where you are." He had told them to buy land, to produce crops, to raise live stock, to send their children to school, to become worthy citizens of a great republic. But the land was so poor, its yield so scant; the hogs were razor-backs; the cows gave so little milk; the children came to school half starved. Their ways of planting and harvesting were the most primitive. Superstitions and folklore so dictated their methods that he could not seem to reach their fundamental needs. He needed help, trained help, scientific help. Alabama was starving. Its peoples, its soils, were going to waste.

And still the rain beat down, rotting the cotton!

Dr. Washington turned from the window and with an air of resolution walked to his desk. He had made a decision. He would write.

Some months before, after he had delivered an address in Cedar Rapids, Iowa, a man had come up out of the audience and, shaking his hand, had said, "I feel it an honor to shake the hand of another educated freedman."

Dr. Washington smiled and murmured modestly, "We are trying to do our part."

"Not all like you. There is only one other—George Washington Carver."

"Carver? Carver?" He had repeated the name. "I don't know him."

"He's the Negro expert in soils and systematic bacterial botany who teaches at Iowa State University."

"A Negro—teaching at Iowa State University?"

"He's a genius, all right. Can raise corn on a wooden floor!" Laughing, the man moved on and was lost in the crowd.

During the following weeks, Booker T. Washington had made inquiries. He could learn very little, but the new catalogue from Iowa State University did carry in its faculty list the name "George Washington Carver, B.S., M.S., Agriculture and Bacterial Botany." It also stated that Mr. Carver was in charge of the greenhouses. Here was the man Washington needed.

But how could he expect such a man to consider coming to Tuskegee? He was sure that this Carver was one of the few Negroes, born and raised in the North, who had had the advantages of family and wealthy influence all his life. Graduated from Iowa State University, what could he know of poverty and want? And now he was earning an excellent salary in a position which carried honor and prestige. He had not dared to write him.

Washington smiled grimly. He needed the man who could "raise corn on a wooden floor!" Alabama clay hardened like rock. Bricks was all *he* could make of it! And so, in desperation, he wrote his letter.

He told this "great man in the North" of Alabama, of slaves now freed and of their children who swarmed over the land. He told him of the school, what its founders had visualized and what he had tried to do. He told of its limitations, its needs, its hopes.

He closed with the words, "I cannot offer you money, position, or fame. The first two you have. The last, from the place you now occupy, you will no doubt achieve. These things I now ask you to give up! I offer you in their place work—hard, hard work—the task of bringing a people from degradation, poverty and waste to full *manhood*."

Four days later, in his laboratory, George received the letter. Even before he had opened the envelope there coursed through his being a thrill of anticipation. He received few letters and this, he saw, had come from a distant state. He read to the end without moving. Then, without a word he went out and walked towards the edge of town. People meeting him on the street smiled and bowed, but he passed on unheeding.

When he reached a favorite spot, hidden from the road and close beside a small stream, he sat down and pulling the letter from his pocket read it again very slowly.

"The children, barefoot, come for miles over bad roads. They are thin and in rags. You would not understand such poverty." George raised his eyes and for a few moments looked down the silent stream. "These people do not know how to plow or plant or harvest. I am not skilled at such things. I teach them how to read, to write, to make good shoes, good bricks, and how to build a wall. I cannot give them food and so they starve."

He read the last paragraph over twice.

Then he pulled a small notebook from his pocket, tore a sheet and scribbling on it three words, signed his name. Holding the sheet in his hand he walked back to the village, stopping at the post office. Here he bought a stamped envelope which he addressed to "Dr. Booker T. Washington, Tuskegee Institute, Alabama." He placed the note inside, sealed the envelope and mailed it. Afterwards he went back to his laboratory and to work.

For several days he said nothing. His mind was occupied with final plans. He knew that his leaving Iowa State University at this time would greatly inconvenience others and upset their schedule. He spent long hours explaining details to his assistant, saw that his notes were completed and all his work in perfect order.

At Tuskegee the letter was received. It said simply, "I will come," and it was signed "G. W. Carver." Nothing else, no date, no questions, no comments. Dr. Washington's heart was filled with gratitude and joy. He waited, content.

At Ames, young Carver had now done all he could. That evening as Mr. Wilson was about to leave the office, George stopped him, "May I see you a moment, Mr. Wilson?"

A certain gravity in tone caused his former teacher and warm friend to look at him sharply. Without a word he closed the door and came forward. George handed him the letter.

James Wilson's face grew sad as he read. His eyes searched George's face as he handed it back. George answered the unspoken question.

"I have written."

Wilson turned away. "It was inevitable! We could not have kept you here."

In a few words George explained what he had done to

help with the change in the laboratory, outlined suggestions and told his plans. To all this Wilson nodded sadly.

"No one can take your place."

The next day they went together to the President of the University. He was dismayed at losing such a teacher, pointing out that George had only just received his Master's Degree, that he was throwing away a golden opportunity. He spoke of the distinction which this position at Iowa State University gave Carver. He acknowledged how much they would miss him.

George was deeply touched. He tried to make the President see what Iowa State meant to him, then he handed him Booker T. Washington's letter. There was a long silence in the room. At last the President rose and said quietly,

"In this life we are prone to turn our eyes away from true greatness, lest we be blinded. He asks you to give up money, position and fame, but in their place he offers—immortality!"

George stood up then. The President took his hand. His eyes were moist as, looking hard into the black man's face, he added the benediction,

"Go—with God!"

And George went out—with God.

10. SALVAGING SCRAP

THE TWO MEN met on the steps of the Administration Building at Tuskegee and for a few minutes stood talking. They were often to stand thus together in the years to come and always they made a striking contrast. Tall, broad-shouldered, robust, deep-voiced Booker T. Washington, with his leonine head, strong features and tawny complexion, and George Washington Carver, slender figure poised lightly on his feet, narrow slightly sloping shoulders, delicate features, high-pitched voice and eyes, the burning center of his dusky face. This was the fall of 1896 and, as he looked out over the school grounds, Carver later confessed that he was appalled, almost bewildered.

"I had never seen anything like it. There was yellow soil and red and purple and brown and riveted and banded, and all sorts of things, except grass or plants. There were erosion gullies in which an ox could get lost!"

Yet a few miles away, beside the railroad tracks at Chehaw, he discovered Neviusia, a rare deciduous shrub which he had been taught grew only under the most careful cultivation.

At the time of Dr. Carver's arrival, Dr. Washington apologized that the carriage had not been at Chehaw when his train arrived.

"I'd forgotten that you might not know about the short line on to Tuskegee. Conductors don't always inform our visitors," he explained.

"The boys told me you sent your fine surrey and best horses to meet all 'big folks'." Carver's eyes twinkled. "They wondered why you bothered today!"

Washington laughed and regarded this young scientist with keen appreciation. His lack of ostentation, quiet, simple dignity delighted him. But he was puzzled also. Who was this man? Where had he come from?

Carver did not consume the time talking about himself. He asked a dozen keen and searching questions which made Washington wonder even more. Then he said he'd like to see the laboratory.

Washington replied at once, "We'll go to the Agricultural Hall. It's our newest building, put up by the students. They," he added, "are mighty proud of it."

"But, the laboratory," began Carver. Washington held up his hand.

"Also—it has plenty of space."

Carver regarded him with a quizzical expression around his eyes.

"I see. You mean you're giving me the space and—"

"God has given you the brains!" finished **Dr.** Washington.

"Well," said Carver, dryly, "I guess, together, we ought to manage a laboratory." And then they both chuckled.

They looked at each other, the chuckle grew to laughter, and the two great souls knit as one. Never in the close companionship, ending only with Booker T. Washington's death, did their understanding, loyalty or faith in one another waver. Not even death changed that. For when the offers came from round the world, with gold and fame and everything men seek, Carver said simply,

"I promised Dr. Washington I'd work at Tuskegee. He's gone, but Tuskegee and work and needs remain."

No laboratory, no greenhouses, no gardens! Carver did not voice his dismay and if he thought with longing of all he'd left behind, no one knew. Quietly he rounded up the few students in Agriculture.

It did not take him long to discover that "farming" was the most unpopular subject in the curriculum. Most of the boys had come to Tuskegee to get away from farm work. They wanted to learn a "trade" or "skill." Anybody could farm! Their frankly expressed attitude is told by T. M. Campbell in his delightful little book, "The Movable School Goes to the Negro Farmer."

"Custom and environment in my home community had schooled me in the idea that all work other than farming could be done only by white people. But when I reached Tuskegee and observed such activities as saw-milling, brick-making, the construction of houses, carriages, wagons and buggies and the making of tin utensils, harness,

mattresses, brooms, clothes, shoes—all done by Negroes—
it was to me like entering a new Heaven. I could scarcely
believe such things were possible."

To make the subject of Agriculture even more undesir-
able, some teachers in other departments sought to punish
students by assigning them to "the farm." But among the
students whom Dr. Carver first met were Jacob Jones,
now a lawyer in Oklahoma, and Walter Keys, who engaged himself to this new teacher as helper, J. H. Palmer,
who served all the remainder of his life at Tuskegee, and
some time later, Thomas Monroe Campbell, first Negro
to be appointed Field Agent in the United States Department of Agriculture, and Sanford Lee, County Agricultural Agent in the State of Georgia.

How was he best to reach these boys who, with no
elementary background, no knowledge of General Science
or even books as taught in northern high schools, wanted
to know how to make things grow? Sanford H. Lee has
described something of Dr. Carver's method:

"My very first recollection of him was my first morning in his class. As he always did, before going right into
the subject at hand, he gave us about ten minutes' general
talk. I remember his words so well—

" 'To him, who in the love of nature holds communion
with her visible forms, she speaks a various language!' All
of us stared at this strange man from 'up north.' What on
earth was he talking about? Then, looking hard at us, he
continued, 'Young people, I want to beg of you always
keep your eyes and ears open to what Mother Nature has
to teach you. By so doing you will learn many valuable
things every day of your life.' How many times have I

heard him quote Bryant's "Thanatopsis" both to his classes
and on other occasions. In fact, it was rather difficult for
him to begin the discussion of any lesson without quoting
some favorite author, or from the Psalms. 'O Lord how
manifold are Thy works, in wisdom hast Thou made them
all.' This was one of his favorites.

"To this day, I seldom begin a day without thinking of
that familiar Bryant quotation—'To him who in the love
of nature—' As a county agent, every year, I learn much
more from my chickens and orchard and flowers than I
do from books. They 'tell' me something every time I walk
among them—just as Dr. Carver told us they would."

The word went out among the students that the new
teacher was "different." Students who had been sent to
"farming" for punishment decided to remain. The first
campaign to salvage waste was being organized!

One morning the new teacher closed his talk with a
little poem. He said it was called "Things not Done Before." Whether he wrote the lines himself or found them
somewhere is not known. The final verses are:

> "The few who strike out without map or chart
> Where never a man has been,
> From the beaten path they draw apart
> To see what no man has seen.
> Their deeds they hunger alone to do,
> Though battered and bruised and sore,
> They blaze the trail for the many who
> Do nothing not done before.
>
> The things that haven't been done before
> Are the tasks worthwhile today;
> Are you one of the flock that follows, or
> Are you one who will lead the way?

Are you one of the timid souls that quail
At the jeers of a doubting crew,
Or dare you, whether you win or fail,
Strike out for the goal that's new?"

His voice lilted on the question and raising his eyes he looked into the faces of his students. They smiled back at him and he said,

"Today, we're going to do something which has never been done before. We're going out and find the things we need for our laboratory. We're going into town and look through every scrap heap. We'll go to the back doors and ask the lady of the house for old kitchen utensils she can't use. We need containers of all kinds, and lamps, and pans in which to cook."

He showed them pictures of crucibles, and beakers, distilling apparatus and extracting apparatus. From his box he took out tubes and small glass cases. "These are the kind of things we need. God knows our need. He will direct us! Shall we go?"

"Yes, sir!" they said, and followed him.

It was an exciting hunt. The students had caught his crusading spirit. They searched up and down alleys, raked through trash and dump heaps, politely but firmly accosted housewives, gathered hollow reeds from the swamp, which "teacher" said could be used for pipettes. When evening came, they met with all their findings. Carver praised each one. What he could not use at once, he set aside, saying,

"There is no waste, save of time. All of these things can be used again." Thus spoke the first and pioneer chemurgist. Only now is the country awakening to the truth of his words.

You may see that first laboratory equipment today preserved in the Carver Museum: a large lantern, its chimney still shining bright; jugs, large and small—one of them marked "Vinegar," a bent skillet, saucepans, broken bottles, tops of cans, an oil lamp, pieces of rubber. With this discarded scrap Carver began to rebuild Alabama.

A twenty-acre patch of ground was assigned to him— "no good" ground. Hogs rooted among the weeds and rubbish on it. He and his students first cleaned it off and then he asked for a two-horse plow. No one down that way had ever seen a two-horse plow, but Dr. Washington okayed his request and one was sent for. When it arrived and Carver hitched it up and began to turn the soil, observers slapped their thighs and rocked with laughter. The idea of a professor plowing! Even his students were a bit chagrined. But he was good-natured about it, even joking with the farmers who gathered round. Their mirth changed to pity, then.

At his bidding, the students brought back muck from the swamps and leaf-mold from the woods. He plowed these under, then told them to clean the barns and bring the "drippings." The farmers were appalled when after all this work, instead of planting cotton, he planted cowpeas!

When the students harvested the spindly cowpeas with a miserable pea in each stalk, they were disgusted. All this for something to throw to the hogs! But the teacher surprised them by saying,

"Now I'll show you how to cook them!"

Well, Northerners were a bit crazy anyhow! But one evening they all sat down to a delicious meal prepared by their professor. Never had they tasted such food. Afterwards, he explained each dish—prepared from cowpeas! The word got around and other students asked to join his classes. People began to talk.

When he planted sweet potatoes on his tract, they simply looked on, saying nothing. But when the tract yielded eighty bushels to an acre, their eyes opened. In the spring he said to his now greatly augmented class,

"Now, we shall see. I've been *rotating crops* on this land. It has been *rested, refreshed* and *enriched*. Now, we'll try cotton."

This they could understand. Long before the cotton was picked, farmers came from near and far to gaze in wonder at the perfect stalks and when he harvested a five-hundred-pound bale of cotton from one acre, whites and blacks regarded him with deep respect. Never had such a thing been done in that vicinity!

Meanwhile, Carver was acquainting himself with the neighborhood. Each morning at four he arose and went to woods or swamp. To the discouraged people of Alabama, he began to say and to write that all around them was untold wealth; that the state had more varieties of trees than could be found in all of Europe—twenty-two species of oak, pine trees, the longleaf, shortleaf, upland spruce, lowland spruce, slash, yellow—all valuable hard woods. The yellow poplar, with its yellowish-green blossoms, often reached a height of one hundred and twenty feet. There were twenty varieties of the white-blooming haw tree, magnificent evergreen trees, rare yellow-blooming magnolias. And that spring he found more wild flowers than he had ever known existed!

When the country people saw him gathering plants and

scooping up different kinds of soil, they said, "This man's a root-doctor!"

And they came to Carver with their aches and pains. He, recognizing that most of them were suffering from the hidden hunger of pellagra, began to prescribe wild grasses and weeds which, tested, proved rich in vitamins. He showed them how to brew teas from certain roots, and cooked and let them taste weeds which grew beside the road. They sang his praises, bowed, and called him "doctor."

They came to him for more advice. He gave it freely and went among them demonstrating how to apply fertilizer. He put into children's language explanations of the interlocked relations of plants and animals and soil and rain and air and sun.

He tested many soils, and because he never threw anything away, the jars and jugs full of clay accumulated and even piled in heaps upon the trays. One bright Saturday morning, Walter Keys, in a burst of energy, decided to clean up for the professor.

He first tackled the dirt in the corner—dumping it all into a large basket. He was just about to carry it out when Carver entered the laboratory. With his hand still on the door, he asked,

"What are you doing?"

"Gonna clean up this place, wash all the tubes, and get everything in order for you, sir."

Walter waited expectantly for his teacher's customary expression of appreciation. Instead, he asked sharply,

"Where are you taking that clay?"

"You've finished with this." Walter was positive. "All of it's been tested, so I'm throwing it out."

"Oh, no," Carver protested, "I—"

What on earth did he want with the clay? He himself wasn't sure, except that— Leaning over the basket, he ran his fingers through the gritty stuff. Slowly, he asked,

"Walter, what do you see there?"

Now Walter had been with him long enough to know that his teacher expected him really "to see." He didn't want to disappoint him, but— He frowned and studied the basket of dirt. All he could see was hard, lumpy, gritty clay of various hues.

"Well, sir—it's—it's got some grit in it, and some's lumpy and some's sort of sandy— Oh, yes," his voice brightened, "there's a few weeds and roots."

"But—the colors—the colors, boy, don't you see them— yellow and red and purple and brown? Why so many colors?"

Walter shrugged his shoulders. He had been looking at similar clay all his life.

"Oh, that! That's just the way clay *is!*"

"But—why?" Carver insisted.

Walter was stumped!

"No," said Carver, waving his hand, "don't throw it out. There *is* a reason. I'll have to talk to God about this."

Walter pushed the basket into the corner. Like Farmer Carver, so many years ago, he was a little shocked. He knew about praying. He knew you should fall on your knees, close your eyes and choose the very best words while you asked God to "forgive your sins," "redeem your soul" and "save" you from "the devil and all his works." He'd heard lots of praying. But he certainly couldn't imagine God "up on His great white throne, bending His ear" to listen to anybody "talking" about clay —not even the Professor!

The Professor had gone out quietly. He was in deep thought. He turned his footsteps towards the swamp and soon the spreading branches of sweet gum trees linked with Spanish moss shut out the sun. The marshy ground tangled with muscadine vines and mosses slushed beneath his feet. But he went on, his eyes catching a glimpse of wild hydrangea, with its spikes of thickly clustered white flowers. How lovely they were! Just then, his foot caught and he fell flat into a mud hole. He was not hurt, but scrambled up quickly. Poisonous snakes inhabited such places and as he wiped away the sticky, oozy mud with his handkerchief, he kept sharp watch. He rubbed hard, but though the mud came off, the stains remained. This was a pretty pickle, he thought ruefully. He looked down at the handkerchief. It was a brilliant blue! He shook the mud off, even rinsed the cloth out in the muddy water. Grit and sand were removed, but the blue remained. For a while he studied it and then said aloud,

"Thanks, Mr. Creator! Thank you very much. At last, I see!"

He hurried back to the laboratory. Walter had gone. Trays and test tubes were clean and shining. Forgetting all about his grimy appearance, Carver pulled out the basket of clay and after arranging a tray dumped a handful of the red clay on it, smoothing it out with his palm. Then, tilting the tray a little, he held a dipper of water above it and allowed the water to slowly drip over the clay. Small rocks and grit began to wash away. He emptied the dipper, and tilting the tray in the opposite direction repeated the process. This he did until there remained on the tray only a thin, pasty coating of red. He touched this lightly with his finger and smeared the finger across a sheet of paper. Holding the paper close to the window he studied it a long time. Then he nodded his head.

"Paint! The people down here are walking on paint—good paint—durable paint!"

For several days and nights he worked alone. He carefully separated his clays according to their colors and washed them clean. Then with intense heat he reduced the clay to finest powder, mixed the powder with oils, with water, hot and then cold, tested them on woods, on canvas, with brush and with fingers. Finally, he told his students.

Shortly after this, a group of white farmers asked Carver to come to their church and tell the people of their community something about soil improvement. The place was some distance away, near Montgomery, but Carver gladly agreed to go.

Walter drove him over, after carefully cleaning and shining the buggy. They found the church with little trouble since it had been described as new and still unpainted. Carver's talk was well received. Many of the farmers came up to shake his hand. One of them said,

"We're poor folks over here and sure needed your talk!"

"I hope I've been some help."

"Our cotton's been falling off steady. We got this church up, and haven't even been able to raise enough money to paint it."

"Now, that's too bad," said Carver, sympathetically.

"Yes, 'tis," joined in another man, "weather's going to come down and our nice building's going to be ruined."

"Is paint so expensive?" Carver was thinking rapidly.

"Down this way it costs a heap. If crops are good this season, I reckon we'll have a rally and raise the money. That'll be after the spring rains, though," the man added regretfully.

Carver smiled at him.

"This is God's house, and it deserves the best. I'll give you paint, good paint."

Several people turned around and stared at the shabby, dark-faced professor. They had heard a great deal about Tuskegee. And they knew the school was always needing money. Yet here was one of its teachers offering to give them enough paint to paint their church. Well! But Carver was speaking gently,

"Lift up your eyes, good people, to the hills of God. See all the gorgeous colors with which he has decked them? We'll take just a little from his bounteous store of pure and lasting coloring, and with it paint your church!"

They really couldn't believe him. But a few days later a little wagon drew up in front of the church. Carver and several students climbed down. From the back they took pails of blue paint, Carver directing everything. And the next Sunday morning the people worshiped in a church which matched the sky in color, its steeple pointing upward proudly. The rains fell and the paint neither cracked nor peeled.

God's good earth gives freely of itself. Nothing is wasted and God's colors do not fade.

11. TUSKEGEE GOES TO THE FARMER

TUSKEGEE HAD MUSIC, such singing as Carver had never heard before! On Sunday evenings the students gathered in the chapel and their voices blended in harmonic beauty that caused the outside twilight to linger a moment and the very birds were still to listen. The fame of Booker T. Washington brought many great people, some from other lands, to study for themselves his amazing theory of "educating hands." They came, curious, condescending, patronizing, and then they heard the children of slave parents singing those songs which had come from out the earth itself, songs old as the mountains, deep as rivers and soaring to the very gates of God! They heard these songs and went away humble and more wise.

Carver never missed these Sunday evenings. "I Gotta Home Inna that Rock"—this was one of his favorites. He felt rather than remembered it. These were the songs his long-lost mother had crooned to him. They lay deep in his heart and spoke to him of hidden roots of strength; of a God "So High Yo' Can' Get Over Him, So Low Yo' Can' Get Under Him, and So Wide Yo' Can' Getta Round Him," a God who sent His chariot "Swingin' Low" to find his "little people."

One Sunday on his way back to the Agriculture Hall after the service, he stopped at the dormitory to speak to one of his students. It was a balmy, spring evening and the student had not returned to his room. Students were snatching these precious moments of leisure and using them as students always have since Socrates first met his classes in the Forum. On his way out, Carver glanced into the "parlor." This room was also empty, but, noting the upright piano in one corner, Carver entered. It had been many months since he had touched a piano. Even before coming to Tuskegee, other duties had crowded out his music. Now he sat down and began to run his fingers softly up and down the keys.

Darkness fell and he played on—snatches from Handel and Mendelssohn interwoven with bits of the Spirituals he had just heard. He played a little prelude, recalling Mrs. Millholland and her hopes for him. No, he had not become an "artist" as they had predicted at Simpson. Here he was merely a "southern farmer," a teacher in a poor, struggling school, a "root-doctor" brewing herbs, a "house painter" smearing mud on walls! Had he failed? No, the sweet assurance came back to him. His fingers might be stiff upon the keys, but he was "bringing life." He made things grow from ground that had been barren, he was "opening the eyes of the blind" and they were finding God in mud and weeds. Beauty was coming now where ugliness had been. Yet he had done so little!

His fingers rested and he leaned his head against the frontal piece. There was so much to do. A sound behind him made him turn. The hall lamp had been lit and there in the doorway stood half a dozen students. Now, they pressed forward.

"Professor! You were playing!"

He was embarrassed and immediately rose.

"Oh! No, no! Play some more!" they begged.

But Carver shook his head.

"I never heard such playing," said one girl, "I—I wish," she stopped.

"What do you wish, my child?" asked Carver.

"I wish my ma could hear you. She like music." The girl was shy.

"You sing in the choir, don't you?"

One of the boys had lit the lamp on the center table and now he could see their faces gathered round him.

"Yes, I sing. That's all the music we have where I come from—singing."

"That's plenty," Carver murmured.

"No, 'taint," disputed a boy. "You could play in our church. All the people would come to hear, from miles around."

Carver laughed. "But—why should I?" He shook his head. "I'm not a musician, I'm a—"

"You said we should give out—what we got—" the girl's eyes glowed softly, "an' you got—music!"

The night bell rang just then and they hurried off.

Lights would soon be out. "Early to bed and early to rise" was the rule at Tuskegee.

Carver walked slowly to his rooms in the Agricultural Hall. He knew that on his early morning trip to the woods he must "talk with God" about this.

For some time now he had refused to face a growing problem. His rapidly expanding department needed money. Increased acreage now under cultivation, the scheme of crop rotation being introduced called for better and more farm implements. He wanted additional live stock and the barns were already too small. Dr. Washington was even then away on one of his frequent trips raising funds for the school. Carver had sat spellbound under Washington's eloquent oratory. The wizardry of his words drew thousands of dollars yearly to Tuskegee. Without envy Carver wished he had his gift. In his musings he smiled. The little girl had said "An' you got music!" Out of the mouths of babes and sucklings—perhaps that was the answer.

Almost timidly he made the suggestion to Warren Logan, treasurer of the school.

"A concert tour!" Logan was enthusiastic.

Carver had merely said he "might give a few recitals on the piano." But Logan's mind leaped forward to all sorts of possibilities. He had ceased to marvel at anything this quiet, thin scientist from up north suggested. All his works had a way of bearing fruit. So not for one moment did he hesitate now.

He wrote circulars and sent them out. They announced simply that "Professor Carver would appear in concert" such-and-such a date at such-and-such a town. They told that Professor Carver was a musician trained at Simpson College, that he had been graduated from Iowa State College and was now on the faculty of Tuskegee Normal and Industrial Institute.

Meanwhile, when he could spare time from classes, laboratory and farm, Carver put in hours of preparation. The students heard him practicing and paused to listen. They too had ceased to question anything he did.

In the years to come there were those who wondered at the full-dress coat and vest with English walking trousers hanging in Carver's closet. He never wore them, and usually merely chuckled when questioned about them. He had had them made for this concert tour.

When school closed for the summer, he set out. He played first in Montgomery, Alabama. Then, avoiding large cities, he followed the Black Belt into Mississippi and back through Louisiana into Georgia. He played in churches, white and black, in schools, halls, sometimes in barns. He played upon battered, old, out-of-tune pianos and sometimes upon reed organs. His repertoire was small, but filled his needs: Handel's "Largo," "The Flower Song," McDowell's "Woodland Sketches," always a simple Prelude and then that interweaving of his own of simple southern melodies.

The audiences liked both the music and the artist.

Now, for the first time, he really saw the South; saw the "hundreds of squalid, ramshackle cabins, tenanted by forlorn, emaciated, poverty stricken Negroes who year after year struggled in cotton fields and disease-laden swamps, trying to eke out a miserable existence. When day was done, they came home to rest in the crude one- or two-room log cabins or houses of rough pine. Often the families numbered more than a dozen persons, ranging from infants in arms to the old and decrepit. In these shacks they ate, slept, and lived. Often only one or two beds. Pigpens often at the very doors. Wells were in many instances down the hill from these pens or close to them. Windows, windowpanes and screens were practically unknown. Steps were a thing of danger upon which to tread. In countless cases no toilets whatsoever, and where there were, they were often just a few boards nailed crudely together with a piece of sack serving as a door." Once he was stoned from a town. His speech betrayed him as a stranger.

About the middle of August, Carver returned to Tuskegee. He had money for his farm implements, but he had much more—a well-defined program was shaping in his mind. Tuskegee must go out to these people. They could not come to it. For long hours, he and Washington sat talking. They walked together and Carver showed him all that had been done.

Since 1892 Washington had been holding an annual Negro Farmers Conference at Tuskegee. To this Conference hundreds came, often afoot, walking long distances, some came in carts drawn by oxen. His aim had been "to bring together for a quiet conference representatives of the common, hard-working farmers and mechanics—the bone and sinew of the Negro race, and its ministers and teachers." Thus he had sought to find out from the people themselves the facts as to their conditions and to get their ideas as to the remedies for the present evils. The Fourth

Annual Conference had established a simple set of rules:

1. To abolish and do away with mortgage system as rapidly as possible.

2. To raise our food supplies, such as corn, potatoes, syrup, peas, hogs, chickens, etc., at home rather than go in debt for them at stores.

3. To stop throwing away our time and money on Saturdays by standing around town, drinking, and disgracing ourselves in many other ways.

4. To oppose at all times the excursions and camp meetings, and to try to secure better schools, better churches, better teachers and better preachers.

5. To try to buy homes, to urge upon all Negroes the necessity of owning homes and farms, and not only to own them, but try to beautify and improve them.

It will be seen, therefore, that Washington's *aims* were high. He had set up the program, but Carver pointed out that the program could not be directed from Tuskegee alone.

"We must go out and *show* them, not only how to produce, but what to produce and then what to do with it," he insisted. "We must build them a house in *their own community* and teach them how *to live in it*. We must take the flowers from the woods and plant them in their yards and prove to them they can keep a cow which will give milk."

To all this Booker T. Washington nodded his head.

And so the first Movable School of Agriculture became a reality. Washington appointed a committee, headed by George Washington Carver, to draw up definite plans for a demonstration wagon, including the kind of equipment it should carry to the very door of the farmer who did not or could not attend an agricultural school. The late Morris K. Jesup of New York made the donation with which was purchased a vehicle to carry exhibits and demonstrations to the homes. The Jesup Agricultural Wagon was fitted up and set in operation in June, 1906, and Thomas M. Campbell, that year graduated from the Agricultural Department, was placed in charge as demonstrator.

The wagon carried a cream separator, milk tester, revolving hand churn, a two-horse steel-beam plow, a one-horse steel-beam plow, a diverse cultivator, spike-toothed harrow, a middle burster, a set of garden tools. Later the cream separator was removed (there was no cream) and in its place was set a large crate accommodating a cow of standard breed. They started out in Macon County only, but news of the Movable Farm School from Tuskegee spread and invitations from white and colored people began coming so rapidly that it became necessary to extend its activities.

The entire story is told by T. M. Campbell, himself. Their arrival in a community was cause for much excitement. They usually stayed three days, using a good central place as headquarters, often the county courthouse. Farmers brought in enough products to keep a standing exhibit. A convenient field nearby was plowed, a garden spot chosen for planting. The demonstration began. Diseases of trees were pointed out, remedies were explained and used, fruit trees were pruned and sprayed. An old, ramshackle house was chosen, repaired and cleaned and in it women demonstrated model home making. They made curtains from flour sacks and wove rugs from grasses and corn shucks. Then they cooked and laundered. Later a nurse (who afterwards became Mrs. T. M. Campbell) was added to the group. She taught them how to care for babies and told them of their proper food and clothing.

Alabama lifted her head! Washington began to see the tangible results of all his years of labor. On every side the cotton was improved; great Tuskegee ran smoothly. He offered to raise the salary of this ardent worker who was making his dreams come true. But Carver shrugged his shoulders and asked simply,

"What will I do with more money?"

Young Emmett Scott, Washington's efficient secretary, later Treasurer of Howard University, overheard and stared at the "simple" Carver in amazement. Never before had he heard a teacher refuse a raise in salary. The man must be crazy!

But Washington turned away smiling. He understood and set to work organizing the Negro Business Leagues. He knew that Carver would not want for anything. The Earth was his.

Carver was busy, but his mind was troubled. The South had too much cotton. Then he turned to raising peanuts!

12.   "AS YE SOW, SO SHALL YE REAP"

THAT SPRING the cotton, all in bloom, was lovely. Many of the farmers had heeded Carver, had "rested" their acres with sweet potatoes, or cow peas, had enriched their soil with fertilizer. But they had quickly turned back to cotton, for in the southland cotton reigned as King. Now the farmers looked forward to the best harvest in many years. Money would at last be plentiful; prosperity had come to Alabama.

And then, one morning they arose, looked out across their fields and gasped with horror! In one night, the lovely blossoms had turned brown, were falling to the ground, the leaves had yellowed and the stalks drooped down! They rushed out to the rows, the women wept, the children stared wide-eyed. The dreaded boll weevil had arrived, a little half-inch worm, and all their cotton crop was doomed.

Years before the boll weevil had crossed into the United

States from Mexico. Texas had fought him back, at times seemed to have succeeded. But every so often now, he had appeared a few miles further north. Now, the boll weevil had come to blast the hopes of all farmers in the Cotton Belt. None could escape. Nothing could drive out this terrible pest until he'd had his fill. Billions of eggs would be left, only to be eradicated from the soil by the strongest poisons, poisons which would also kill young cotton seeds!

Back in Tuskegee, Carver heard the cry which went up all about him. He had few acres in cotton and his peanut vines stood green and sturdy in the sun. The boll weevil did not touch them! Here was food for thought. Already, he knew much about the peanut. Now he organized his facts and with his findings went out into the stricken countryside.

"Plow under your cotton!" His voice was like a clarion call. "Spray the soil with poison and one month later plant peanuts!"

The people heard him, but were not comforted.

"Peanuts!" they said. Their name for them was "goobers." "Goobers are food for hogs, good enough to chew. But all our income crop is gone. We're ruined!" they wailed.

"No! No!" Carver grew more emphatic. "The peanut is an ideal food for man. Plant peanuts!"

He prepared a bulletin and sent out hundreds. The bulletin declared:

> Of all the many crops grown by Macon County Farmers, perhaps there are none more promising than the peanut in its several varieties and their almost limitless possibilities.

Of the many good things in their favor, the following stand out as the most prominent—

1. Like all other members of the pod-bearing family, they enrich the soil.
2. They are easily and cheaply grown.
3. For man the nuts possess a wider range of food values than any other legume.
4. The nutritive value of the hay as a stock food compares favorably with that of the cow pea.
5. They are easy to plant, easy to grow and easy to harvest.
6. The great food-and-forage value of the peanut will increase in proportion to the rapidity with which we make it a real study. This will increase consumption, and therefore must increase production.
7. In this county two crops per year of the Spanish variety can be raised.
8. The peanut exerts a dietetic or medicinal effect upon the human system that is very desirable.
9. I doubt if there is another foodstuff that can be so universally eaten, in some form, by every individual.
10. Pork fattened from peanuts and hardened off with a little corn just before killing is almost if not quite equal to the famous Red-gravy hams, or the world renowned Beechnut breakfast bacon.
11. The nuts yield a high percentage of oil of superior quality.
12. The clean cake, after the oil has been removed, is very high in muscle-building properties (protein), and the ease with which the meal blends in with flour, meal, etc., makes it of especial value to bakers, confectioners, candy-makers, and ice cream factories.
13. Peanut oil is one of the best known vegetable oils.
14. A pound of peanuts contains a little more of the body-building nutrients than a pound of sirloin steak, while of the heat and energy-producing nutrients it has more than twice as much.

The bulletin gave details on cultivation, harvesting and

preparing peanuts for market, with an added word regarding peanut hay.

The farmers read and listened and took new hope. Perhaps everything was not lost. Perhaps these "goobers" they'd been feeding to the hogs had more about them than they knew. At any rate, the things this dark-eyed man from Tuskegee had told them before had turned out well. They took his word and planted peanuts.

The first crop was good. Enough was bought up by the market and what remained was utilized, following Carver's instructions. By this time he had sent out other bulletins containing many ways of preparing peanuts as a food. He told them how to make peanut bread and cake, mock chicken, sausage, cheese and roast, candies, and that delicacy rare in the south—ice cream.

And so more farmers planted peanuts.

There was no market. Up North no one had ever heard of cooking peanuts and they had all the bags of salted peanuts they wanted. Vendors were well supplied. The price on peanuts fell to almost nothing. They rotted in the fields. Catastrophe which for the time had seemed averted again faced the farmers of Macon County and this time all because a "fresh young upstart" from "over Tuskegee way" had told them to plant peanuts!

The people, white and black, who had begged him for advice and help, now heaped their condemnations on him. That year they called him "nigger," and wondered why they'd ever been so stupid as to listen to him.

The ways of God and man are strange! Carver, wounded to the quick, withdrew into his laboratory and shut the door. He refused to see anyone. He blamed himself utterly. He had made a terrible mistake. He should have foreseen this disaster. In his despair he lifted his stricken eyes to God and asked,

"Oh, Mr. Creator, why did You make this peanut? What is it? What can we do with it?"

And in the stillness of the night, God answered him.

Carver called for heaped-up bushel baskets full of peanuts. And when they brought them, he shut the door again. They saw his light burning throughout the night, took him trays of food which he scarcely touched. To those who tapped lightly on his door, he called out in a queer, brusque voice,

"Go away! We're busy!"

They looked at each other wondering who could be in there with him. None of the students, that was certain; no faculty member—not even Dr. Washington.

Six days and nights passed and on the seventh, Carver staggered from the laboratory, climbed the stairs to his room, and fell across his bed. He slept until the dawn of the next day. Then he rose, took his customary walk in the woods, returned and ate a hearty breakfast.

Only then did he say to his few selected boys, "Come with me!"

They followed close at his heels. When they entered the laboratory, they could only stare at the many bottles and containers on the table. Where had he gotten milk and cheese? And when he named the other articles, their wonder grew. There were about two dozen products in all. Before his death, he had found three hundred in the peanut alone. But this was the beginning. Now he knew his way!

In a lecture several years later at Minneapolis, he gives his own description of that session with God.*

"I asked, 'Dear Mr. Creator, please tell me what the universe was made for?'

"The great Creator answered, 'You want to know too much for that little mind of yours. Ask something more your size.'

"Then I asked, 'Dear Mr. Creator, tell me what man was made for.' Again the great Creator replied, 'Little man, you still ask too much. Cut down the extent of your request and improve the intent.'

"So then I asked, 'Please, Mr. Creator, will you tell me why the peanut was made?'

" 'That's better, but even then it's infinite. What do you want to know about the peanut?'

" 'Mr. Creator, can I make milk out of the peanut?'

" 'What kind of milk do you want, good Jersey milk or just plain boarding-house milk?'

" 'Good Jersey milk.'

"And then the great Creator taught me how to take the peanut apart and put it together again."

On that occasion he drew forth from his box of samples a continuing procession of face powder, printer's ink, butter, shampoo, creosote, vinegar, dandruff cure, instant coffee, dyes, rubberoid compound, soaps, salads and wood stains.

"The great Creator gave us three kingdoms, the animal, the vegetable and the mineral. Now, he has added a fourth, the synthetic kingdom."

To get the scientific explanation of what Carver did at

* "The Man Who Talks with the Flowers," by Glenn Clark, Macalester Park Publishing Co., St. Paul, Minnesota, 1938. Used by permission.

this time, one must leap forward to May 7, 1935, when in Dearborn, Michigan, some three hundred men and women gathered in what was called the first National Farm Chemurgic Council.

At this conference "synthetic" was defined as meaning "the reconstruction of decomposed substances" and "chemurgy" as "an organized attempt to create true wealth—the only real wealth which lies dormant and neglected in the powers of the soil and air and sun and mighty minds of people. 'It is perhaps less a new thing than a new way of looking at old things.' "

In his tiny laboratory in the deep south, Carver began this process of "decomposing substances" and "combining minute particles to create new wealth" long before the renowned work of William Jay Hale, Charles Herty, Francis Garvan or Harry Barnard. Later Henry Ford was to pronounce his chemurgic credo:

"I forsee the time when industry shall no longer denude the forests which require generations to mature—but shall draw its material largely from the annual produce of the fields— The time is coming when we shall grow most of an automobile—the farmer will raise the raw materials for industry."

Christy Borth in his "Pioneers of Plenty"* calls George Washington Carver the "first and greatest chemurgist."

"He merely took the goober apart chemically, separating the water, fats, oils, gums, resins, sugars, starches, pectoses, pentosans, legumen, lysin and amino acids, spreading them before him, trying endless shufflings of the parts under varying temperatures and pressures. Out of

* From "Pioneers of Plenty," by Christy Borth, copyright 1939, 1942. Used by special permission of the publishers, The Bobbs-Merrill Company.

those shuffling came a crop-use that is now putting $45,000,000 a year into peanut farmers' pockets—$200,000,000 a year into the peanut business.

"Here was chemurgy before chemurgy was a word. Here was transmutation of waste into wealth."

Today in the center of the main street of Enterprise Coffee County, Alabama, may be seen a monument to a bug. It was placed there in 1919 by the people of the community who raised $3,000 to pay for it. The monument bears this inscription "Profound appreciation of the boll weevil and what it has done as a herald of prosperity."

The boll weevil had driven the farmers to raising peanuts!

But sweet potatoes were rotting in the fields. And with his eyes now opened to new possibilities, Carver turned to them. In all, he extracted from the lowly yam more than a hundred products, most important being flour, starch tapioca, breakfast foods, stock foods, numerous dyes for silks and cotton, crystallized ginger, vinegar, mucilage, ink and—much later—synthetic rubber!

It was during the first World War that the United States Government learned that at Tuskegee Institute, thanks to Carver's genius, they were saving two pounds of wheat a day by using sweet potato flour with wheat flour and, upon testing, enjoying a better loaf of bread than before. They sent for Carver and he went to Washington with his sweet potato exhibit and sweet potato flour, promptly adopted as useful, helped to feed the millions of American soldiers and their allies.

Booker T. Washington did not live to see the complete exoneration and triumph of his most idealistic and untiring worker. Before his death, he had released Carver from all classroom teaching, shielded him from intrusion and provided him with all the limited means the school could afford. In November, 1915, while on a speaking tour in the north to raise more money, he was stricken. He died November 14th.

A nation mourned his loss and at Tuskegee, George Washington Carver wept for his friend.

13. THE MIRACLE MAN AT HOME

THE LETTER caused some comment in the office. The envelope was long and very thick, rich cream in color. The stamp and postmark of Great Britain could not be missed. The boy delivering mail balanced it in his hand. He hoped the Professor was not thinking of going over there to help out in the war. That was possible! No one saw Carver open it and no one knew its contents until he dictated a reply. He wrote thanking the "Royal Society for the Encouragement of Arts, Manufactures and Commerce of Great Britain" for the honor they had conferred upon him by making him a member of this distinguished body. He said he did not deserve the honor. This was in 1916.

News of his appearance at the Senate for the Smoot-Hawley Bill got out and he was besieged with invitations from various colleges and organizations to speak before them. He accepted where such a talk could do some good.

Never did he turn away from service, but always he sought to avoid mere ostentation.

In 1923 the great ones called him to New York and pinned the Spingarn Medal on his shabby coat. He was embarrassed and with a murmured word of thanks sank into his seat. He still felt more at home with the "little people" of the woods.

He lived now in a two-room suite in Rockefeller Hall at Tuskegee. These rooms became his castle. His living room was "always just a little crowded." It was, in fact, a confused combination of picture gallery, library, hothouse and museum, with a small wood stove in one corner upon which he brewed his herbs and developed the many new recipes for various kinds of dishes made with nuts or roots or weeds. Bookshelves on three sides reached from floor to ceiling. Here were books on geology, agriculture, botany, chemistry, physics, astronomy. Books about butterflies, mushrooms, frogs. Here were books in English, French, Latin and German. There was the complete set of "Internationaler Kongress por Angewandte Chemie" published in Berlin; "A Comprehensive Survey of Starch Chemistry" by R. P. Walton; "The Chemistry of Synthetic Resins" by Ellis; "Technology of Cellulose Ethers" by E. C. Warden; "Chemical Technology and Analysis of Oils, Fats and Waxes" by Lewkowitsch. These were a few of the well-thumbed volumes. He did not scorn the works of other scientists, but read everything thoroughly "in order to keep pace with the scientific thought of the day."

"Life requires thorough preparation," he constantly cautioned his students.

To the day of his death he spoke of himself as a "student," a "seeker after wisdom."

A large table stood in the center of this room. On it were piled rocks and stones and stalactites and stalagmites and scores of other formations which only a trained geologist would recognize. By this time he was convinced that many useful products could be dug from the very rocks and stones. Outside the window on a great shelf stood plants and flowers.

The first thing that one saw on entering the bedroom was his mother's spinning wheel which stood beside the window where the sun could shine upon it. No particle of dust was allowed to rest anywhere on spokes or stand. He tended his rooms himself and wiped it carefully each morning with a soft cloth. On the little stand beside his bed were found the books he liked to touch early in the morning or the last thing at night—the Bible, "The World's Great Religious Poetry" by C. M. Hill, and frequently letters of great men. Among this lot was Bishop's "Theodore Roosevelt's Letters to His Children."

He spent his spare time doing needlework, inventing his own designs. His patterns of lovely filet crochet can be matched only in the best shops. The story is told that one of the women teachers complained of not being able to find a certain type of lace panel for a new dress. Carver asked her to describe what she wanted. A few days later he presented her with a panel of exquisite beauty. It was fitted into the front of her dress and drew attention by its delicacy and fine workmanship. The dress wore out. Not a thread of the panel had drawn or broken. When the dress was discarded, the teacher returned the panel to Carver and he placed it in a case with other pieces of embroidery, tatting and crocheting.

Six of the friends and co-workers always ate together at a table in one corner of the huge dining hall. They had all known and loved Dr. Washington, and a meal seldom passed that they did not speak of him. These table-mates always exchanged Christmas presents. One of the last notes written by Dr. Carver is treasured by Myrle Cooper, Superintendent of the Greenhouse at Tuskegee. It is dated December 4, 1942. Dr. Carver was confined to his bed, but as Christmas approached he wrote: "Please send them a little plant as usual." Then came their names: "Mrs. W. T. Shehee, A. D. Long, Celia Watkins, S. P. Martin." These were the table-mates still left. The note was signed "Yours very truly, G. W. Carver."

His choicest gift was flowers. He painted them and reproduced them in paper and wax with such lifelike perfection that it was said, "You never know whether the flower Dr. Carver is wearing is real or artificial."

He always wore a flower.

His clothes were a source of irritation and vexation to all who loved him. At this time it was said he was still wearing the suit in which he had arrived at Tuskegee. That may have been true. The story persisted even later. He made his own ties, mended his shoes, patched his pants and sewed the rips in his coat. He preferred being taken by visitors for one of the neighborhood farmers. It saved his time and spared him from embarrassment. He never mastered the art of small talk and would often chide students,

"You never saw a heavy thinker with his mouth open. Stop talking so much."

But he never wished to be considered rude and his innate gentleness would cause him to go to much pains to avoid hurting anybody's feelings. At one time it came to his ears that he thought himself "uppity and better than other folks" because he had failed to attend any of the large receptions or social functions to which Mrs. Booker T. Washington and other ladies of the faculty constantly invited him. At the next large affair given by Mrs. Washington he closed his laboratory, went to his room, donned his full dress coat and walking trousers, cut a fresh rose for his lapel and walked across the campus to the Washington home. Students nearly dropped in their tracks!

When at his ring the door was opened, he reached into his pocket, drew out a card and handed it to the pop-eyed student maid.

"Aren't you coming in, Mr. Carver?" she managed to gasp. She anticipated the excitement his entrance would cause.

But he shook his head.

"No, I'm only calling to pay my respects. I must work late tonight at the Agricultural Hall."

Then Carver went back, took off his full-dress outfit, put on his sack coat and patches and, hunching his shoulders, returned to work.

He was neighborly and enjoyed nothing better than serving his friends with some of his new dishes. The Walcott children living in the big house down the hill from Rockefeller Hall would often see him coming with a steaming crock. They'd run in calling to their mother,

"Here he comes, mamma, with something else for you to taste!"

Good-natured Mrs. Walcott never failed him.

"Though," she says, "I took some awful chances! He always had the pleased enthusiasm of a child learning new things, saw something fascinating in each rock or weed or piece of clay. Every few days he'd make discoveries, any one of which could have made him rich and famous. He'd tell them to me with delight and glee, then walk for miles to find out why some poor farmer's crops were failing, give him a cure and come back through the woods, finding some rare, sweet flower or brightly colored stone!"

Money was not so plentiful those days. Cotton had dropped from the high war prices, farms were deserted and help hard to find. With cotton going to waste, Carver began producing insulating boards, cordage, paper and rugs and finally paving blocks from cotton which might have rotted in the fields.

His findings began to attract commercial eyes.

Then, in the spring of 1928 Carver received a letter from President John L. Hillman of Simpson College. Simpson College invited him back to commencement that year. They wanted to confer upon him the honorary degree of Doctor of Science. President Hillman wrote: "When I consider the difficulties with which you had to contend, I am simply amazed at what you have accomplished. Our college honors itself by conferring on you this degree."

He held the letter in his hand a long time and his mind went back through the years. They did not seem so long.

He had done a little. He lifted up his eyes and saw—not hill tops. Only magnolia trees in bloom, the climbing honeysuckle, acres of peanuts and, beneath his feet, red clay!

PART III

AND THE FULLNESS, THEREOF

14. "GOD'S LITTLE WORKSHOP"

It was set up in the new Milbank Building—a modern chemical laboratory, not very large and furnished only with the bare necessities. But far in advance of the former work bench. Each item had been carefully chosen by Dr. Carver himself.

"There'll be no money wasted on fooldoodlings!" he had said severely.

He was as excited as a boy when it was finished. Secretary Emmett Scott joined him in the doorway. Early morning sunshine flooded the clean, fresh room.

"This would have been a glad day for Mr. Washington!"

Secretary Scott knew so well how much Carver had accomplished with so little. He knew how he had justified Washington's belief in him and now looking down the shining table with its polished tubes and gleaming beakers,

Secretary Scott was happy that at last Tuskegee had given him equipment. He rubbed his hands enthusiastically.

"We've come a long way!"

Carver had gone forward. Leaning over, his eyes intent, he tested the focus of a small microscope. His shabby coat hung loosely from the stooped shoulders, and, with a little start, Emmett Scott noted gray hairs above the hollow temple.

"He's getting old!" This was his thought, but aloud he said, "Now, you'll perform miracles!"

Carver's hand trembled slightly as he lifted a tiny tube and, holding it up so the sunshine could go through, said quietly,

"Only God performs miracles. Here, I'll only listen for His voice, and try to carry out His instructions."

And, taking a handful of clay from a jar behind him, he spread it on a slab and fitted the miscroscope to his eye.

The room was very still as Mr. Scott turned, softly closed the door behind him and walked away.

The Secretary was puzzled and a little worried. He realized that all these years George Washington Carver had remained a stranger to them. He wished Mr. Washington had lived. He could have explained Carver to Tuskegee.

Was Carver a genius—a giant, walking among them, but towering so far above that his head was lost in the clouds? Was he a religious fanatic or a profound philosopher? Or was he merely an eccentric scholar, clever, a bit conceited, now becoming a bit cantankerous as he grew older? The outside world was beginning to heap honors upon him. More and more frequently was he being called to Washington, consulted by the United States Department of Agriculture. Hardly a week passed that he was not invited to speak at some college, before scientific groups, clubs, Chambers of Commerce. Southern newspapers were mentioning him with pride; the Crown Prince of Sweden had come to see him. A Crown Prince at Tuskegee, remaining two weeks, daily in long conferences with Carver! Not until he had gone away had the other members of the faculty known—and they had resented their exclusion. Even more keenly had they felt the slight when the Prince of Wales came. Everyone knew how this visiting heir to Great Britain's crown had captivated Washington. When it was reported he had expressed a desire to visit Tuskegee, no one had thought he meant only Dr. Carver! But it turned out that the Prince wanted to talk of plants and flowers and peanuts with this man! They had joked together, laughed at the same things—a Prince, so soon to give away a heavy crown and Tuskegee's "quite ordinary Mr. Carver," a son of the soil, born into slavery!

Tuskegee could not understand. And what people do not understand they are apt to dislike. Tuskegee did not know what Dr. Carver was doing.

He worked alone. While others were still sleeping, he arose, walked for a time in the woods, returned to his laboratory and there "alone with God" he carried on his research. People distracted him. They asked questions, the answers to which he was even then seeking. He had no time for comments or idle speculations. He wanted the Truth, the whole Truth. He could not use scientific terms to his unprepared and unschooled students at Tuskegee. When it was absolutely necessary to speak, he used only the simplest words. They said he did not talk like a scientist!

Carver talked little. He saw everything.

His approach to his work was not unlike that of Louis Pasteur, who, finding analogy between fermentation and disease, passed on to germs as the essential cause. Carver, observing nature, took his cue from her. He watched a spider weave her web and said:

"It had six spots on the underside of its body. Also little spinnerets which it used in making web. As I watched it began to weave. First, it made five or six little balls and pitched one in this direction and one in another until it had thrown them all out. These silklike threads going out from the center acted as guy ropes. Then the little spider in the center began to weave in and out. It performed the task accurately, perfectly, and symmetrically. I decided to make a web, began it with fine silk, but it was not nearly as perfect as the spider's!"

These words are from the notebook of a student. This was his morning lesson. Carver continued his lecture by telling his students that God had given them as great intelligence as He had to the spider. Therefore, when they did not succeed at first, they must continue trying until they *perfect* methods.

He observed that cows, sheep and elephants employ their own peculiar methods of transforming grass and so produce milk, and ivory, and wool. The silkworm provides man with ideas for today's synthetic textile fibers. It did not seem too much to him to set about finding methods to break down component parts, reorganize them and so transform the products of the soil to other needed products. Like Pasteur, he leaped forward to his goal.

"Researches on primary causes are not in the domain of Science, which only recognizes facts and phenomena which it can demonstrate," the Frenchman had said many years before.

Pasteur, surrounded as he was by a host of other minds, exchanged, discussed, criticized each finding. He could lay his works before the *Academie des Science*. But Carver had no circle of discussion in which he could try his wings —nothing. He was a black man set apart. Realizing certain barriers, he himself further retreated into this solitude. Friction would have destroyed his usefulness. He wanted to do the maximum of good for his own people.

Secretary Scott recalled the time when Thomas A. Edison sent his personal representative to ask Carver to join their staff at Orange Grove, New Jersey. The representative had repeated Mr. Edison's words,

"Together, we shall unlock the universe. Your limited facilities where you are, delay and hamper you. Here we have everything with which to work."

How true that had been! And Carver had listened quietly. Then he had been both kind and gracious, humble before the offer.

But his answer was final. "They need me here."

Then he went on to tell how he had promised Booker T. Washington to do what he could towards "changing poverty and waste to full and useful manhood."

"I can do my best work here at Tuskegee—here, where I cannot depend on many assistants and expensive gadgets," he had added when they pressed him.

Repeatedly he was later asked, "How much did Edison offer you?"

He grew somewhat annoyed with the question. Finally, he gave out to the press: "The salary ran to six figures."

Secretary Scott pondered on how much could have been done with a salary of not less than a hundred thousand a year!

Carver did not call himself a scientist. The term was applied by others. L. J. Pammeau, plant pathologist, considered him a "systemic botanist of rare ability." And Myrle Cooper, now Director of Tuskegee Greenhouse, says,

"I never saw a flower, plant, tree, vine or weed he didn't know. He identified them instantly."

Everyone knew that his detection of plant diseases was uncanny. With keen perception and minute attention to details, he "saw" where others were blind.

And sometimes he saw unexpected things.

One day a student brought into the greenhouse a carefully wrapped package which he said had been given him by a lady in the village. She had told him her geranium was suffering from a peculiar ailment which was killing it. She asked that it be taken to the "plant doctor" and if possible saved.

With the greenhouse assistant, the boys unwrapped the parcel and were about to examine the plant when Dr. Carver entered the building. Wrappings were tossed aside and the boys were eager to begin their analysis. But Dr. Carver stopped just inside the door. Something was wrong. Before anyone could speak, he moved quickly over to the bench, stooped and picked up the pieces of string which had fallen or been thrown on the ground.

"What's this?" His voice was sharp with displeasure. "Someone *cut* this string!"

There was a moment's silence, then one of the boys said, "Yes, sir. I—I—couldn't untie the knot."

"Let's see your fingers!" The boy held out his hands.

"Um—um—" Dr. Carver was examining each finger, carefully. "I see nothing wrong here. You were in a hurry, so you waste string and paper."

He dropped the boy's hand and was now carefully pulling out the pieces of string and rolling them into a tiny ball. The students knew his rule—string was never thrown away under his eagle eye, but always rolled and carefully preserved for future use. And packages were always untied, so that the wrapping cord remained whole. As Dr. Carver rolled the string, on this particular morning, he continued his little lecture on economy. Suddenly he stopped. He was staring hard at the string.

"What's this?" They saw nothing.

"What, sir?"

"Here on this string. Don't you see it?"

He held the string out for them to see. It was a little damp from contact with the wet paper about the plant, but other than that his students detected nothing. But he was excited. Laying this bit of string out on a sheet of paper, he rolled the paper carefully and hurried away. They knew he was going to his work bench. They looked at each other. Anything might happen! Later, he explained to them.

On that string he had detected a peculiar mold. It was quite different from anything he had ever seen. He was sure of that. At the laboratory, he put the string under a microscope. No, he could not find it listed as a mold which attaches itself to fibers, yet here it was. Therefore, he made slides and sent them with his own description of the pathogene causing the disease to Washington. In a few days the answer came back. This disease was extremely rare, had been found only once before in England, never in America. It caused destruction of cotton cellulose and, had it not been checked at once, might easily have ruined cotton crops in this country for many years to come.

Carver had seen it on a bit of string.

"*Is* he a genius?" Secretary Scott asked himself the question as he entered his own office.

As time passed, more and more people began to ask that question when Dr. Carver's name was mentioned. Some refuted the fact, almost angrily, as if he had made such an assertion. Others—

When, in 1929, A. F. Woods, director of the scientific work of the United States Department of Agriculture, declared that science was "opening up a field of chemical research greater even than the coal tar chemistry of recent years," the *Montgomery Advertiser*, a leading Alabama newspaper, said proudly on December 23, 1929:

"In this connection, Alabama can boast that it has a man who has probably done more in this field of research and who probably knows more about chemical possibilities of plants than any other scientist in the world. That man is Dr. George W. Carver, the great Negro scientist of Tuskegee Institute."

It was with no feeling of pride that the "great Negro scientist" early one morning was squinting through the yellowish, thick liquid smeared in a test tube. He had been working all night and still the problem confronted him. Now, across the campus sounded the second and last bell for the six o'clock breakfast. Carver sighed deeply and wiped his hands on the already spotted apron. He was very tired and he was discouraged. He really didn't want any breakfast, but he held himself rigidly to the rule of eating at meal time. He knew his body was frail and needed nourishment. A good cup of coffee would help. A cup of coffee! He stopped for a thought had struck him. Why not? Why not test it out? Why not get some help as to what was wrong?

He chuckled to himself and, breakfast forgotten, moved with feverish haste. Of course it was the thing to do. It took but a few moments to pour some of the thick liquid into a small container. Then, his cap set at a rakish angle, he hurried out and across the campus towards the dining hall. Late students observed him with surprise. Dr. Carver was noted for his punctuality.

They were all seated when he reached his place. Mr. Palmer regarded him severely as, with a hasty "Good morning," he slipped into his seat. As the oldest of the table-mates, Mr. Palmer could and did express his disapproval.

"You're late!"

Dr. Carver's keen eyes quickly noted several things. Coffee had not yet been served. But there on the table, close to the sugar bowl, sat the small pitcher of fresh cream. He was thinking rapidly.

"Aren't you feeling well this morning, Mr. Carver?" There was maternal concern in Mrs. Watkins' voice, as she leaned forward.

"Why, yes, ma'am. Yes, ma'am, I'm feeling fine."

Somehow—some way—he must draw their attention away. It would only take a minute. He was staring out the window behind them.

"Then, why—"? began Mr. Long.

"I'm surprised they didn't make you late, too. Could you believe they were possible?" Carver's eyes now were wide with his surprise and his voice piped with excitement. The expression on his table-mates' faces was one of bewilderment. He leaned forward eagerly.

"You saw them, didn't you?" he asked.

His table-mates looked at him in astonishment. "Saw who?"

"Saw what?"

"What are you talking about?"

It was now or never. Carver pointed dramatically out the window.

"Quick! It's not too late. You're just in time to catch the mist before it rises. Look, over there to the left—"

They had all risen now and were pressing close to the window. Behind them Carver was working rapidly. An empty pitcher from the serving table close by was exchanged for the full pitcher on the table. Then the pitcher was no longer empty, because he had poured the contents of his container into it, all the time talking rapidly.

"I never thought much of those impressionists until I saw them for myself. . . . But, it's true. They really are

pink." He approached the window now and asked guile-
lessly, "Can you see them?"

The ladies were still straining their eyes, but Mr. Palmer
was annoyed.

"What in heaven's name are you talking about, Mr.
Carver?"

"The haystacks—the haystacks over there beyond the
barn."

He was looking out the window now. "They are—no,"
he corrected himself, "they *were* pink. Earlier this morning they really were pink!"

Earl Wilson, a newcomer, wanted to laugh. He re-
strained himself as he observed the stricken look on the
faces of the ladies as they all sheepishly returned to their
seats. Mrs. Shehee protested.

"I never heard of such foolishness!"

Dr. Carver's voice was very serious as he explained.

"That's because you're not up on your French painters,
Mrs. Shehee. I'll lend you some books on the subject. You
see Monet—or was it Manet—said that in the early morning
haystacks appeared to be pink and he—"

"Bosh!" exploded Mr. Palmer. "Let's eat!"

Dr. Carver regarded him with a pained expression which
intensified as Mr. Palmer held his cup for the waitress to
fill it with steaming hot coffee. A spoonful of sugar and a
generous portion of "cream" poured from the little pitcher
completed his morning routine. Then, he lifted the cup to
his lips. The cup was lowered almost immediately. He
was frowning.

Mrs. Watkins was stirring her coffee and staring at it.
Mrs. Shehee called sharply,

"Waitress! This cream is sour!"

Wilson had come to the same conclusion. Certainly the cream had curdled in his cup, but oddly enough the cup of coffee gave off an odor which reminded him of—peanuts! He decided to taste it. As he raised the cup to his lips he suddenly realized that Dr. Carver was watching him, his eyes fixed intently. And then he knew. Something to do with peanuts had gone into that coffee. The taste was unmistakable.

"Do you like it?" Carver's voice was anxious.

"No, sir," Wilson was positive, "I do not."

Carver sighed deeply. The waitress had come up and Mrs. Shehee, reaching for the pitcher, started to explain.

"The cream is—"

But, Dr. Carver's hand stopped her. He moved the pitcher himself, saying,

"It's no good. There's the cream on that side table. Young lady, will you bring it back here?"

"But, I—" the student waitress started.

"Never mind what you did—I moved it!"

The others were all regarding him now. They began to understand and tasted their coffee, experimenting.

"What would you say was wrong with it?"

They were a little flattered that Dr. Carver should consult them. Yet their coffee was ruined!

"Well," began Mrs. Watkins, slowly, "it's just too much peanut—that's the main thing. It isn't cream!"

"Yes," Carver agreed, "all the elements of cream are there but my combination is still just—peanut."

The newcomer wanted to ask questions. "You made this —this liquid from peanuts, didn't you?"

Carver nodded his head.

"Then, how could you expect it to taste like anything else but peanuts?"

Dr. Carver regarded the new faculty member, his eyes seeming to bore through him.

Then he asked sharply, "Does butter taste like grass?"

Before the young man could catch his breath, Carver had left the table and was walking hurriedly across the dining hall.

"You mustn't mind him, Mr. Wilson. He's just like that," Mrs. Watkins explained.

"Imagine him going to all that trouble so that he could change the pitchers!"

"Pink hay stacks! What was he talking about?"

"He's crazy."

"Oh, no," Mrs. Watkins interposed quickly. She turned to Wilson, "Don't let anybody tell you Dr. Carver's not a smart man. That cream made from peanuts wasn't good, this morning. But, he'll keep working on it—and he'll get what he wants. You'll see!"

And Wilson had reason to recall her words. For the cream which Dr. Carver finally developed from peanuts did not curdle, nor did it in any way resemble peanuts. Flavor and quality were identical with the best A-grade cream!

Earl Wilson had come to Tuskegee to work in the newly opened bank. By this time the Institute had become a little town all to itself, with its power plant, post office, library, church, shops and now the bank which handled all financial matters for the school. And here Mr. Wilson was to learn much more about Dr. Carver.

It was several days after the incident of the cream that Wilson, looking through the grill of his bank window, observed Dr. Carver silently waiting. It was almost closing time and so he hurried to serve him.

"I need my check." Carver's eyes smiled almost apologetically.

Wilson hesitated. He knew that faculty salary checks were paid from this office, but they went out the first of the month and it was now only the twenty-third.

"I'm sorry, Mr. Carver, the checks aren't—"

He was interrupted. "Young man, you're new. You don't know what you are talking about. Call somebody who does."

One of the clerks stepped up to the window. "Just a minute, Mr. Carver. I'll get your check."

Wilson turned away, slightly annoyed. He observed the clerk open a drawer in the safe. It seemed full. The clerk took out the pile, drew a check from the bottom and carefully replaced the others. Returning to the window he shoved the check under the wicket to Dr. Carver, who, without glancing at it, merely said "Thank you, sir" and stuffed it into his pocket. Instantly he had gone.

The clerk looked at Wilson and grinned.

"Don't look so glum, my friend. You'll learn!"

Wilson bit his lips. "What is there to learn and why should he get his checks before the first?"

The clerk laughed. "That's a good one! Come, I might as well show you now as later."

Again he opened the safe drawer. "You see this drawer full of checks?"

"Well?" Wilson nodded.

"All of them are made out to George W. Carver," the clerk explained.

"Oh, I see. This is his additional money. Well, I knew he made money off his inventions and—"

The clerk shook his head. "You're wrong. They're all salary checks. Look!"

He emptied the drawer on the desk and picked up the check which had fallen from the bottom. "This is the next one in order to give him. Look at the date."

It was marked May 1, 1915!

Wilson stared, unbelieving.

"Yes, he's just drawn his April check. When he comes again, he'll want the May check."

"But—but—this is 1923!"

"Sure," grinned the clerk, "soon we'll have to open a new compartment in the safe—just for Carver. They come every month!"

"You mean to say he lets his checks lie here for years?" asked the bewildered man.

"Try and get him to take them. Please do."

"But—what does he use for money—?"

"Well, it's sure he doesn't have any tailor bills out." (He lowered his voice.) "They say he came to Tuskegee wearing the same clothes he has on now!"

"I don't think such joking is funny."

"Well, if you look in the books, you'll see he's drawing the same salary he did the first year he came to Tuskegee."

"That's a shame," began Wilson indignantly, "a valuable man like—"

"What's a shame?" inquired the clerk. "He won't accept a raise. They've offered them to him—many times."

The clerk was replacing the checks in the safe. "And if you think this is trouble—wait till that check comes back from the bank in Montgomery!"

A week later, he waved the slip of paper at Wilson and said, "Here it is! Now, for the treasure hunt!"

They entered the huge vault together. There from the dusty files they drew the large check book marked April-May, 1915. Turning the pages they found the stub corresponding to the check in their hand. The check was pasted in and the book returned to the "morgue."

"When I left Alabama in '25, Dr. Carver had not yet drawn all his checks through 1916!" says Earl Wilson, today.

"The Earth is the Lord's!" While people all about him prattled of money, toiled for money, sweated for money, hated because of money and died in the attempt to get more money, Carver, from some Olympian height, grew to possess the earth! To him, money was a mere convenient, easy medium of exchange. He used it as he needed it. Most of the time he did not need it.

This was neither a pose, nor an affectation. Fabulous sums offered to draw him from Tuskegee presented no temptation. He had all the money he needed. After that, what did it matter?

"What would I do with more money?" he asked the question in all earnestness.

The peanut farms of several wealthy growers in Florida were visited by a blight which was destroying their crop. They sent Carver specimens of the diseased vines. He told them what was wrong and how to cure it. After his diagnosis and treatment had proved correct, they sent him a check for one hundred dollars, promising they would send the same amount thereafter monthly as a retaining fee. By return mail Carver sent back the check, telling them God did not charge anything for growing peanuts and he could not charge anything for curing them.

Later, an industrial group, adopting his process for converting wood shavings into synthetic marble, offered him a huge salary to run the laboratory. He refused, and the manufacturers moved to Alabama, getting his advice free.

"But think of all the good he could have done with all the money he refused!" many people have exclaimed.

No doubt, lesser men could have done much with the money Carver did not take. But not Dr. Carver.

He was a sojourner in the world of men. Material things would have weighed him down. He was poised lightly on this earth, his wings untrammeled by earthy concerns. Houses and land, bank accounts and insurances, diamonds and gold—lesser men need these things for security. George Washington Carver did not.

A cot upon which he could lie down and rest. God's earth from which he could draw all-sustaining strength. The golden sunshine and the glisten of dewdrops in the early day. These things he had, and more—

A sheltered place where every day, alone and undisturbed, unhurried, he could work—could dream, and plan to improve the good earth, to increase the yield, to open secrets now locked in the earth, to make a better place for men to dwell.

This was the shop where he could work with God!

15. "TAKE 'IM TO P'FESSAH CARVER"

THE TWO BAREFOOT BOYS moved in a swirl of dust as they kicked their way along the dry, dirt road. Overalls were hitched up over miniature smooth shoulders, burnt black by the mid-summer Alabama sun. Ragged straw hats gave some protection to the small, narrow faces. One of them clasped in his thin, bare arms a dog. Obviously, the dog was heavy, for he held it awkwardly. They might have been ten and eleven, perhaps older. Black boys in Alabama do not grow so rapidly.

There was little shade along the road. On either side lay open fields green now with cotton, not yet burst into bloom. Here and there moved bent figures. They were "chopping" the plants.

The boys had been walking a long time and were silent, reserving their strength for this last mile. As they reached the top of a rise in the land, they paused and drew deep sighs of relief. For not too far ahead of them lay the end of their journey—Tuskegee. They could see the buildings and grounds spread out in a beautiful green and white pattern. And there was the red of new brick buildings, the shining reservoir of water, the towering smokestack.

Heaven must be like that!

"Yo' sho they gonna let us in?" The boy holding the dog doubted such good fortune.

The second boy spoke with confidence, "Sho."

Then, to clinch the argument, he asked, "Ain't mah brothah there?"

They started down the hill at an accelerated pace. But the smaller boy, with his load, began to pant,

"Reckon yo' could tote Putch again for a spell?"

"Reckon."

No words were wasted. The transfer was made, the two boys handling the dog tenderly. Notwithstanding their precautions, the dog whined and kicked out once as if in pain.

The first boy, released from his burden, rubbed his arms and shook his shoulders as they started again.

"Fur a lean hound, Putch sho is heavy," he commented.

"Sho is," agreed the second, endeavoring slightly to shift the dog's weight, but at a whimper he gave up.

"Ain't much further now, Putch," he comforted. His voice was hoarse and dry. "Yo' gonna be *runnin'* back!"

The smaller boy's eyes lit up and then clouded.

"What if tha man ain't there?" he asked.

"He'll be there."

They reached the village and rested for a little while in the shade of a building. Then they were at the gates of

Tuskegee Institute. Even the confidence of the larger boy was now somewhat shaken by their impressive size. He had entered them once before with his older brother, but now— They hesitated, peeping around the huge side post.

A cadet, spying them, called out, "What you two boys want?"

They came forward, trembling a little.

The older boy swallowed. "We come to see P'fessah Carvah?"

The cadet eyed them severely. He recognized their mission.

"Your dog sick?"

"His leg—he can't walk—P'fessah Carvah will make 'im well."

"He's a fine dog," the smaller boy added quickly. "Mah pa say—"

A cart was approaching the gate. The cadet hailed the driver.

"Hey! Walt! Going up by Mr. Carver's place?"

"I'm going over to the farm. Why?"

"These two boys taking their dog to Mr. Carver. Couldn't you drop them on your way?"

"Sure. Hop in, boys!"

They reached to take the dog from the tight clasp, but he growled menacingly.

The boy chided him. "Shut yo' mouth, Putch! Can' yo' see we're goin' to P'fessah Carvah?"

A couple of hours later the two boys leaned back against a post on Rockefeller Hall porch. They were content and rested and fed. They had talked with "P'fessah Carvah." When he had lifted the dog, it had not whimpered or growled at all. Wide-eyed and silent, they had watched him bathe and oil and rub the bad leg. Then, under his instructions, a big boy had made a soft bed and they had left Putch comfortably asleep. "P'fessah Carvah" was going to keep this pet right there until he was all well. He promised to write when they could come for him. A letter! The small boy wiggled in excited anticipation!

They themselves had been taken to another building where, seated on high stools, they had eaten their full of grits and side pork and greens and corn bread—real corn bread, baked in an oven! Then they were told that the farm wagon was going out that afternoon and they would be dropped off at their own place. Now all they had to do was—sit. It was wonderful! Tuskegee was wonderful! And "P'fessah Carvah—"

The smaller boy broke the silence. "Ah been thinkin'."

"'Bout what?" It was a foolish question, but seemed necessary.

"Ah reckon God look jus' lak P'fessah Carvah!"

The older boy pondered a moment. He'd always thought about God as being very, very large, sort of sitting on great banks of white clouds and talking louder than the thunder. He couldn't imagine "P'fessah Carvah" in that position! But as he considered the brightness of those deep, dark eyes, looking at him and sort of smiling—how Putch had looked up at P'fessah Carvah as he turned and pulled his leg—how those long, brown hands had touched Putch and the sound of singing in his voice as he spoke so softly—as he thought of all these things, he turned and smiled,

"Ah reckon so, too," he agreed.

So, they came to him—young and old, white and black. They called him from other lands. Russia wanted him there to assist with the Five-Year Plan for Agriculture. Mine owners in Mexico begged him to join them in that country. The West Indies asked his help towards increasing the kind and nature of their products. From far and near people found their way to Tuskegee. They came, bringing specimens of worn-out soil and hard clay asking him to "fix it." They came with blighted plants and he restored them. One day they brought him a boy with a withered leg.

By this time Carver was certain of the healing properties inherent in peanut oil. Under his skillful massage, with the aid of that oil, he had rubbed away many pains and aches, had restored and strengthened muscles. But this boy had infantile paralysis.

Carver made no promises, but set to work.

At the Third National Chemurgic Council, meeting later at Dearborn, Michigan, he showed slides of the boy's leg as it was when he was brought to Tuskegee, then a series of successive slides showing the leg as the boy was later able to shift from crutches to cane.

"And now," Dr. Carver told them, "that boy is playing football at college."

There was a moment of breathless silence. Then someone said,

"Maybe it was the rubbing."

"That might have been it," conceded Carver, smiling. "I was the official 'rubber' at Ames many years ago."

"Would you say the peanut oil cured his paralysis?" he was asked.

"I do not know. I only know I've been using it ever since and in each case there has been improvement."

In December, 1932, the story appeared in the newspapers. "Carver discovers cure for Infantile Paralysis!" Dr. Carver promptly issued denials, which went unheeded. He was deluged with letters, telegrams, long distance telephone calls, begging him for the "cure." Frantic parents brought their crippled children to him. They came in long lines of automobiles from dawn until after dark. He devoted all his week-ends to treating these cases. All day Sunday he would work—rubbing afflicted limbs with peanut oil!

Records show that of the two hundred and fifty cases which he treated, all recovered to some extent—some wholly. Yet, medical authorities have never yet agreed whether the healing lay in the oil itself or in Dr. Carver's hands. He was not a medical man and therefore could make no authoritative statement and others seem loath to assume that responsibility. Laymen and *The Montgomery Advertiser* pleaded to both doctors and Governor Bibb Graves of Alabama to exhaust "all possibilities of peanut oil as a remedy for infantile paralysis epidemic now in Alabama."

Dr. Carver refused all patent rights to the oil and made it available to druggists for sixty-five cents a half gallon. But it would have taken a factory to have turned out the many gallons and barrels demanded.

The idea of going into business never seemed to have occurred to Dr. Carver. He encouraged others to do so, however. In May, 1930, the Carver Penol Company had been incorporated under the laws of Delaware to handle

oil and medical formulas for colds which Carver had per-
fected. To some extent this company now tried to furnish
peanut oil for rubbing, but Carver himself remained completely apart from that effort.

Shortly before this time, scientists at Johns Hopkins
University had enlisted his aid in developing a food for
babies in tropical countries where milk was not available.
This was the kind of work he loved. In a few days, the
vegetable formula was ready—a powder containing life for
millions of starving children or for soldiers camped on
desert wastes.

Powder containing life—not death!

When the authorities at Johns Hopkins learned that Dr.
Carver was coming to Baltimore to speak at Morgan College, a Negro school on the outskirts of the city, they
decided to honor this modest Negro scientist who had
refused both money and publicity for his valuable contri-
bution. They planned a banquet for him and sent out
invitations to leading educators and scientists in that section of the country. Among those to receive the square
white card was Edward Wilson, Registrar of Morgan
College.

He could hardly believe what he read. Johns Hopkins
was inviting him, a Negro, to a dinner party given in honor
of another Negro!

When they ushered the speaker into the chapel that
morning, some of the Morgan College students snickered
at the green-black alpaca coat, patched trousers and old,
broken shoes. Then he stood up and in his high-pitched
voice began to talk.

"When you do the common things of life in an uncommon way, you will command the attention of the world."

It wasn't what they had expected.

"Creative genius is what makes people respect you. It's not a question of color—it's a question of whether you have what the world wants."

He talked on, lifting articles from the large wooden case, explaining how many of them had been made from "things you throw away"—peanut hulls, corn shucks, cotton waste and weeds.

"Ye shall know the Truth and the Truth shall make you free."

They would not let him sit down. They applauded, cheered and whistled. And when order was restored and chapel dismissed they crowded round him, anxious to shake his hand.

The banquet at Johns Hopkins was to be that night. Wilson left his office early and dashed home. Hardly was he in the house before he called out,

"Did my—?"

"Yes, dear," his wife replied, "your suit's hanging in the closet all pressed and ready."

He hurried to his room. On the bed lay dress shirt, white socks, studs. He fussed over each article. Everything must be correct.

He cut himself when shaving.

"Dear, you've plenty of time," his wife remonstrated. But she was excited, too. This was an event!

The beautiful, softly lighted chamber on the university campus pulsated with a sense of high anticipation. The proud South was lifting her shining head above those barriers she herself had raised. Tailors on Bond Street and

Fifth Avenue had attired the guests and as Edward Wilson looked about the room, he squared his shoulders, conscious that his coat set well.

Exactly on the moment the double doors opened and a faultlessly dressed Negro entered. There was a slight movement forward. This must be Dr. Carver. But no,

"I'm Dr. Carver's secretary."

He turned. Behind him Dr. Carver had slipped into the room. Wilson gasped! He wore exactly the same alpaca coat, baggy trousers, the same old shoes and—no—the shirt was fresh and clean, but it was just a shirt, with colored, woven tie. They were too polite to stare.

Dinner was announced.

"I didn't know what to think," says Edward Wilson. "My head was whirling. It was an effort to unfold my napkin. I felt humiliated!

"But in a few moments a ripple of amusement went around the table. They were all bending forward, hanging on his words. I'd missed the joke, but now I listened.

" 'I understand you have worked out a diet for Mahatma Gandhi,' said one.

" 'Yes,' answered Carver, 'I have had that privilege. He is a man of God, but very frail. I know that out of the earth grows every strength he needs.'

" 'Gandhi eats no meat,' somebody murmured.

" 'It is not necessary,' replied Carver. 'From God's earth he can draw his physical strength. The circle is complete. God is in everything. There can be no creative genius without him.'

" 'But—Edison—they say he was an atheist.'

"Carver's eyes flashed.

" 'An atheist! Little, conventional people whose prayers do not reach the ceiling call Edison an atheist because he does not define God exactly as they define Him. I have correspondence with Edison that I prize as I do that with Gandhi. Edison knew as does Gandhi that all knowledge came from the Creator.'

"There we were," Wilson continues, "in our stiff shirts and tight collars . . . My shoe was pinching . . . and there he sat at ease, comfortable, relaxed, thoroughly enjoying the excellent meal, one moment discussing problems of the universe, the next telling a funny story. I watched the twinkle in his eyes as he looked down the table at us and all at once I realized that behind that mild, sweet face there lurked a Jovian wit. He was laughing at us and our petty prides and pomps—our stuffed shirts!

"But, because he was so truly great, he warmed and made us laugh with him."

But on another occasion, Carver did not get off so easily!

In 1933, the Tom Houston Peanut Company decided to present to Tuskegee Institute a bronze plaque of Dr. Carver.

It was to be a great event for the school. The chorus rehearsed diligently. Dr. Robert R. Moten, who had succeeded Booker T. Washington as head of the Institute, invited guests not only from all over the state, but from Atlanta, New Orleans and Washington. Everybody was elated except—Dr. Carver.

The committee on arrangements turned troubled eyes on the shabby figure as, with the utmost unconcern, the man about to be honored shuffled through his busy days. There was much whispering and putting of heads together.

Finally, these faculty members approached him. They talked of what this honor meant to Tuskegee, of the inspiration it would bring to thousands of students, not only on their campus, but throughout the country, of the distinguished guests. He listened patiently, his head cocked slightly sideways, his eyes all the while on a wilting weed beside the walk. Then—

"Dr. Carver, won't you please wear an academic robe—with the doctor's hood?"

He looked up brightly. "I haven't one."

"Oh, yes, you have."

"But—"

"We've ordered one for you. It came this morning!"

The day arrived, the auditorium was packed, the speaker made a long and eloquent presentation speech. Carver, fanning nervously, half suffocated in the voluminous folds of that robe, tapped his shoe impatiently. The applause continued and Dr. Moten bent over and told him he must respond. Looking around frantically, Carver sank further back into the enveloping billows. Two professors approached and begged him to stand. As he did so the applause became deafening. Finally it died away and there stood the great scientist, an annoyed and embarrassed old gentleman, fussing with the front of his robe, over which he was certain he would trip if he took a step forward. He gave up.

From where he stood he said distinctly,

"I never wore one of these things before." He shook a handful of the robe at the audience. "I'll never wear one again."

Gathering up the folds about his thin legs, he left the platform, went back to his room, let the robe fall to the floor, emerged in his comfortable old coat and slipped away to his laboratory.

Only the privileged few—teachers, students or visitors—ever entered Dr. Carver's laboratory. Whoever entered must be first of all an earnest seeker after Truth, not a mere idle curiosity seeker. As the work became heavier, the question of an able assistant in the Experimental Department became more and more imminent. Several promising students were tried out, but none of them quite satisfied Dr. Carver. At one time Macio Thomas, young teacher of chemistry, seemed chosen. During a brief illness Dr. Carver discussed plans with him, but as soon as the sick spell had passed and the flour sack apron again donned, the idea was forgotten.

Carver was now past seventy. Though the exact date of his birth was not known, he had been at Tuskegee forty years. He was busier than ever. He still rose at four o'clock, went first to the woods, returned, ate his breakfast and then to his laboratory. He received baskets of letters daily. People wrote him from all over the world and he insisted upon reading and answering each letter. Many replies he wrote with his own hand, but two secretaries were kept busy taking dictation, sorting and filing his mail.

When in 1934 Dr. Fred D. Patterson became president of Tuskegee, he set himself immediately to convince Dr. Carver that he must accept help in his laboratory research. Some fitting man must be found who could be trained to follow him. For a while Dr. Carver turned a deaf ear.

Then Carver was asked to serve as Collaborator, Mycology and Plant Disease Survey, Bureau of Plant Industry in the United States Department of Agriculture. This meant additional responsibility and so he promised to consider someone.

Dr. Patterson had in mind a young student at Cornell—Austin Curtis, Jr., now graduated and teaching Agriculture at a college in North Carolina. And he sent for him.

Austin Curtis, born July 28, 1910, grew up among the hills of West Virginia where his father, Austin Wingate Curtis, is Professor of Agriculture at West Virginia State College. At the close of the War between the States, his great grandfather had given most of the land upon which to start this school. The young man's work had stood out at Cornell University not only because of his studious application, but for an ease and keenness of perception and vision of application.

The fall session of 1935 was about to start at Tuskegee and teachers and students were assembling. That mild September morning when Carver arose at dawn and set out for the woods, he was somewhat troubled. His frail body was no longer rested when he got up now. Rarely did he glance into a mirror, but this morning he did. Yes, he was getting old. His hair was white, his shoulders bent. He had heard that his assistant had arrived the night before. What was he like and would he really "see"? So few people did.

"The sands are running out, Mr. Creator," he murmured as he threaded his way down the lane, "I'm old and a little tired. I don't want to be disturbed."

Over his head some wild geese called. He looked up.

"So soon? They're coming south for winter. Means they know it'll be very cold. They know what's coming and so they prepare."

He chuckled. "Funny how we use less sense than birds and animals. I know and yet I grumble. Forgive me, Mr. Creator. The work is yours and yours to send the man to carry on."

He returned two hours later bearing in his arms some shrubbery—a *Croton Alabameses*, evergreen with close-fitting scales, silver on their underside, a rare and precious find. He was happy and when he went to breakfast had forgotten his misgivings. There was an air of gaiety in the dining hall. Faculty members and students who had not seen each other since June were greeting one another with shouts of delight. Then, after they were seated, someone nudged Carver and whispered,

"There he comes, Dr. Carver. There's your new assistant."

He looked up. Four or five young men had just entered the hall and stood hesitating at the door. It was obvious they were all new. He scanned them anxiously. Which one? As they moved forward, one figure held his attention—tall, well set, with a pleasing smile as he turned to his companions. But it was the eyes which drew him—keen, deep-set eyes. They were the eyes of one who "saw."

Carver leaned over and said, "That one—I hope *that's* the one!"

Just then, at a nod from a waiter, "that one" moved away from the others and coming directly to his table, held out his hand and said with sincere deference:

"Dr. Carver, I'm Austin Curtis."

Afterwards, they walked together to the office. The young man was disturbed because the great man said so little. Only: "What are you interested in?" "What do you plan to do?" and "Well, look around, get acquainted. I'll let you know when I need you." Then, he was dismissed.

Was he accepted?

He had heard much regarding Dr. Carver's eccentricities and yet—

"I'd never seen a kinder face," Austin Curtis says today. "It was more than kind. Later I knew the quality I recognized that morning was—godliness. There is no other word."

But that September morning he walked away wondering. He had never been in Alabama before and he was attracted by the plant life about him. He saw red clay and thought of the paints Carver had drawn from them. From a magnolia tree over his head he picked a cone with its red seeds. Some of the seed crushed in his hand and, as he wiped his stained fingers, he wondered idly if Carver had thought of using them for paint.

The thought persisted and several evenings later—Carver had not yet sent for him—he slipped into the laboratory and began experimentations. Time passed. It had grown dark outside, but Austin Curtis paid no heed. Nor did he hear the door open, or know Carver was behind him until, as he held the glass tube high squinting at it.

Then the question came, close to his elbow, "What is it?"

Without turning his head, Curtis answered, "Paint." Then, suddenly realizing, he did turn and stammer, "I—I—"

"From what?"

"Magnolia seeds. I—"

Carver took the tube. Now, holding it in the light and peering through, he asked severely, "Did you ever hear of anyone making paints from magnolia seeds?"

"No, sir. But—it's quite clear that—"

The chuckle stopped him. A hand pressed on his shoulder and, "You'll do, my boy. You'll do!" For the first time Carver had there behind his closed laboratory door another "seeker after wisdom."

They became inseparable.

Carver told others what Curtis was doing, pushed him into the foreground, depended on him. When he himself was called to West Virginia for a conference with Governor White, Curtis accompanied him.

"He has developed paints from the magnolia, coffee grounds, Osage orange and in addition to research work on peanuts and sweet potatoes, has conducted independent research on low cost paints and supervised a fiber research project," the Professor said, proudly.

In an effort to find a cheap source of pigment for rural school children, Austin Curtis developed what is now known among artists as "Curtis Browns." They are obtained from magnolia cones. First the cones are ground to a fine powder; next inoculated with bacteria and allowed to ferment for a period. The fermentation process is stopped and the pigment extracted by means of crystallization. Twelve shades of brown are found.

"I am content," Carver had said, proudly.

He called his assistant "Baby." And "Baby Carver" his name became on Tuskegee campus.

16. GOD'S VICTORY GARDENS

GEORGE WASHINGTON CARVER had plowed deep and turned the furrow well. He had sown good seed and carefully tended its growing. Now in the time of great need, his work was bearing fruit. For the world was at war and all the destructive agencies of war were loosed on bewildered humanity.

"With the victims of war thrown out of equilibrium in so many different ways, almost a new book will have to be written and followed up carefully in order to patch these victims or restore them to normalcy. In all this, chemistry must play a major part."

These were Carver's words, spoken before the *Herald Tribune* Forum in New York City, where he had been called to receive the Roosevelt Medal. The citation said, "For distinguished service in the field of science, to a scientist humbly seeking the guidance of God and a liberator to men of the white race, as well as the black."

It was a great honor, but Dr. Carver hardly had time
to receive it. All the roads he had followed for so many
years now emerged and brought him to the place where
a great American could serve the world.

The year was 1939. No bombs had yet fallen on Pearl
Harbor, but men of science were already well aware of
the important role they must fill in a world where Hate
and Greed would, for a time, destroy and twist the brain
of man to do their will.

Ersatz, the science of substitutes, of which so much is
heard in this war, is not the creation of Hitler or any of
his predecessors so much as it is the invention of George
Washington Carver. How did Dr. Carver, the creator of
the new science of chemurgy which is the production of
industrial raw materials on the farm, happen to be the
first man to create a complete system of substitutes for
precious or non-available articles? The explanation is to
be found in the peculiar situation in which he found himself when he left the faculty at Ames, Iowa, to answer
Booker T. Washington's call in Alabama.

In Alabama Dr. Carver found his people in need of
everything and without the means of acquiring anything.
His guide was the needs of the people. His only materials,
what they had. His goal, to make everything they needed
out of what they already had. The result, the creation of
some one thousand items of food, clothing, building materials from the products of a soil that would no longer grow
the one crop to which it was accustomed, cotton.

His sweet potato flour had helped to feed armies during
the first World War and when it seemed that the United
States was dependent on Germany for aniline dyes, Carver

206 DR. GEORGE WASHINGTON CARVER

had come forward with his vegetable dyes. He obtained over five hundred dyes from fruits, leaf, root and stem of twenty-nine plants. These dyes are used on leather, cotton, wool, silk and linen and do not fade in washing or in light.

Now it had become apparent that the United States must serve as a vast reservoir of food and clothes, planes, tanks, strength and good will, for all the world. Carver intensified his work. There was so much to do.

He said repeatedly, "There is no need for America to go hungry as long as nature provides weeds and wild vegetables which serve not only as food, but as medicine."

And so he began to tell people about weeds!

"A weed," Dr. Carver said, "is just a plant growing where it should not grow. Therefore, you pull it up and throw it away. But nature scatters billions of seed. The stronger survive; the weak, untended, die. So these wild plants may have vitality and strength superior to those which have been carefully cultivated."

Here was a "new way of looking at old things." He called attention to weeds which grow in every field, beside all roads, in vacant lots and beside country doors, weeds rich in vitamins, tasting good, many with definite medicinal properties. He listed and described them—wild lettuce, chicory, giant thistle, rabbit tobacco, curled dock, beet root, lambs quarters, black mustard, stock—and told how they could be boiled, seasoned with meat or butter or, better still, pointed out that the shortage of meat or high cost of butter need not matter. For a cup full of fresh peanuts boiled right along with the vegetables will season as well as the side of bacon people in the South were accustomed to use. He suggested that the next time spinach or water grass was served that the housewife substitute a portion of peanut butter on top the steaming dish in place of creamery butter.

Bulletins went out from Tuskegee Experimental Station explaining how to make delicious salads with chickweed, silk weed, white clover and alfalfa and pies from curled dock, sour grass and old-fashioned sheep sorrel. A list of these bulletins is given in the Appendix of this book.

From the beginning, Carver had preached thrift, conserving and preserving. "Throw nothing away. Everything can be used again!" How often they had heard him. Now, all the country was listening. He didn't use the word "dehydrate." Instead he talked simply of "drying food."

"At no period in our history is it more important that every acre, yea, every foot of land be made to produce its highest possible yield. It is equally important that everything possible be saved for our consumption. The shortage of tin cans, glass containers, the high price of sugar as well as the containers, make it emphatic that we have some other method within the reach of the humblest citizen. Drying is without doubt the simplest and best method of preserving a number of fruits and vegetables." He gave out lists and methods showing "how easily and cheaply they may be taken care of."

An example is this recipe for "Strawberry or Peach Leather."

"Take thoroughly ripe strawberries, mash to a pulp, spread on platters and dry in the sun or oven; when dry, dust with powdered sugar, and roll up like a jelly cake, cut into suitable sized pieces and pack away in jars. Peaches may be treated exactly in the same manner. This may then be eaten as a confection or soaked in water and used for pies, shortcake, sauce, tarts, etc. The powdered sugar is a matter of taste and may be left out if desired."

Carver sent out recipes, also listed in this book's appendix, for drying apples, grapes, figs, corn, okra, sweet potatoes, pumpkins, string beans and for making soup mixtures and other miscellaneous—as he calls them—odds and ends. And nowhere does he mention expensive "dehydraters" or other "equipment." Dr. Carver showed people how to use the ordinary cook stove, simple wire frames, mosquito netting and God's abundant sunshine.

It was during these busy days that Carver met Henry Ford. The meeting proved auspicious for black man and white. They became warm friends. For the two of them—the powerful industrial multimillionaire and the simple worker, who daily suffered insults and indignities—nevertheless had much in common.

They were probably born the same year. Both had left the farm, restless, searching, working their way, driven by some consuming urge. That the white boy's way was somewhat easier, that the sight of a clumsy, steam-driven engine moving on the road was the inspiration of his lifework, that he moved through privation, poverty and mockery until at last he devised the first Ford car—these are but matters of circumstances. The passion for work was not yet satisfied, his ideals not yet reached. Henry Ford was still searching. All that he had heard of Carver, the constant diligence, the ceaseless toil, the unconquered spirit—these things intrigued him. At their first meeting, there was mutual respect in their hand clasp. Carver bowed with all the old world courtesy, but there was a twinkle in his eye, a smile upon his face which said, "Here is a Man I'm glad to meet."

Instinctively, Ford recognized that here was a man whose modesty lay in an ego only matched by his own—an ego that identified itself with all the universe and which doubles, triples, infinitely multiplies the personality. With his God, the Earth belonged to Carver. Therefore, he had no wants.

Both of them believed in the benefit of Work. Neither believed in any set hours for work. Ford with his millions had never learned to "waste time"—neither had Carver. Neither could quite understand the philosophy that says man works to eat, but spends his life doing "other things." Perseverance, thrift, frugality were parts of the very woof and pattern of their lives. And Ford had often been heard to express his contempt for money. Often he had told young people that there was nothing of real value or permanent importance that money could buy. Carver, therefore, exemplified much that Ford had said, but which, by the circumstances of his own life, could not prove.

Certain of their similarities showed in their faces. The black man's skull was the larger, but the same deep-set eyes, eyes of passionate dreamers, burned beneath high foreheads; the lower portions of the faces clearly belonged to men who asked a thousand questions. Ford's thin, delicate fingers had the same exquisite skill and efficiency of manipulation as Carver's. Both were poised lightly as if ready to take off for flight.

So they became friends. And friendship to two such men meant work and more work, now doubled in interest because of mutual sharing.

Already Henry Ford had gone far in the development and experiments with soy beans. Close to the Ford Engineering Laboratories in Dearborn are thousands of acres of bean fields. These soy beans represent a step in Ford's program towards permanent plenty. His experiments along this line have been very encouraging. In the laboratories of Ford's plants, men skilled in chemurgy are converting soy beans into innumerable useful products. Carver was intensely interested in all that he heard.

Shortly after their first meeting, Carver accepted Ford's invitation to visit Dearborn. He spent some time there and upon his return immediately turned to several new experiments using soy beans instead of peanuts. Soon he had turned out a plastic material which Ford was able to utilize in certain parts of his cars.

With his interest now drawn to the South, Ford bought a large tract of land fifteen miles from Savannah, Georgia, and transformed the miserable section with its impoverished white and Negro tenants into a huge, busy, prosperous farming acreage and experimental station. Hard woods were cut down in the swamp portions, two schools were built—the one for colored children called "Carver's School"—farmers were supplied with equipment, model homes were erected and acres of goldenrod were planted. The goldenrod was to be used in experiments for producing rubber!

Carver planned this project with him. Carver's clay paint was used on the buildings. He showed the people how to utilize every bit of material on the land, designed and planned special features for their houses.

They enjoyed this work together, trying out new ideas,

discarding those which did not get results, turning wasted lands and peoples into ways of usefulness.

Ford's visits to Tuskegee were never heralded. The morning his private car was seen on the railroad siding at Chehaw they would know he was there. The campus respected his privacy and did not intrude. They let the two old gentlemen spend hours together behind closed doors, talking, talking, laughing—or walking through the woods, dreaming and planning a better world.

"They even liked the same things to eat," says Sam Qualls, a former student at Tuskegee. "I used to wait on them in Dr. Carver's rooms. They took the same amount of cream in their coffee!"

Now, for the first time and in spite of his failing strength Carver left Tuskegee and, accompanied by Austin Curtis, entered a special laboratory equipped for him at the Ford Motor Company in Dearborn, Michigan. Newspapermen gathered round. They sought out Henry Ford, but he would make no statement. With only a few chosen assistants, Carver worked behind closed doors. When he was finally accosted, he said only that "the laboratory would try to find new uses for agricultural products."

The newspapers hinted at rubber, but were given no confirmation.

Carver was leading men to turn back to the earth—God's earth for their needs. What better labor of love could he perform? There must have been times when Henry Ford found himself a little lost. He had grown so used to the power of his money and here was a man who wanted nothing.

Ford built a house for him. It might have been a castle.

What Carver suggested was a simple log cabin, as like as possible to the old log cabin that had been his mother's. Because of Ford's deep reverence for his own mother's memory, he understood. He searched the country for the finest hardwoods, assembled logs from every state in the union and there in Greenfield Village built the "Carver House."

It was a small log cabin that cost a fortune. And Carver was delighted. He worked now with a kind of feverish urgency. He frequently spoke of himself as a "trail blazer." Without complaint he accepted the role. "If only I can build the bridge," he was heard to say. He was willing to leave the rewards of his labors to others.

He saw clearly before him a new era in which "there will be produced from crops grown on the farm, products superior in quality to items in use today, possessing features demanded as a result of modern trends, the restoration of purchasing power and economic balance between farm and industry; making available to a large group necessities that would not be otherwise within their financial grasp."

Many men must be trained, unlimited research must be undertaken, more and more equipment would be needed. He had shown the way. Now as he approached his eightieth year, Austin Curtis drew up for him plans for the establishment of the Carver Research Laboratories. Word was sent out giving the details for the establishment of a Foundation. The large brick building next to Dorothy Hall at Tuskegee was remodeled and converted into the Carver Museum. Here were gathered samples of the work of over fifty years—nearly a thousand articles extracted from peanuts, sweet potatoes, discarded waste and weeds, his precious bottles, handiwork, lace patterns—all the things which George Washington Carver had gathered to him through the years.

His paintings occupied a large room. A booklet describing these paintings was compiled with a foreword by Austin Curtis:

"It is the soul expressing itself when the artist builds a world of his own creations. In creating his world, Dr. George Washington Carver has combined all the forces of life which seem to him significant and worthwhile."

Carver had not gone to Paris and become a great painter, as once he had dreamed of doing. Somehow, he'd been too busy. Instead, during his spare time at Tuskegee he had painted, using Alabama clays and his fingertips instead of a brush. He had done these pictures to show his students that it could be done. But now those paintings hung upon the gallery wall and visitors marveled. And one of them "Four Peaches" was purchased by the Luxemburg Galleries in Paris. Someday a freed France will admire and love this small, exquisite piece. Carver's favorite in this group was a landscape—sunset on a quiet stream of water.

His friends begged him now to rest, to "take it easy." But the spirit of the man was indomitable. His work was not yet finished. Then, one morning in the Tuskegee Chapel, an announcement was made which startled the country. In a quiet voice, before faculty members and student body, Dr. Patterson read these words:

"I, George Washington Carver, hereby create and endow the George Washington Carver Foundation with all I possess, my life's savings of thirty-three thousand dollars."

Having given all his life to "making something where there had been nothing," having dedicated his hands to "creating life," having kept his promise to Booker T. Washington to "lift a race from degradation to full manhood," it now seemed he was giving back to the institution what it had paid him for his services.

But Dr. Carver knew that he was planting more rich seeds in the gardens of time.

17. "ALONG THIS WAY"

THE LARGE, SPOTLESS KITCHEN in Dorothy Hall was warm and fragrant with the odor of coffee and frying bacon. Cooks and waitresses moved with quiet and organized efficiency. Miss Sims, dietitian, was checking the contents of the pantry. Behind a tall screen in one corner, Sam Qualls laid a white cloth on the small table drawn close to an open window.

"Couldn't you close that window, Sam?" Minnie paused with her tray of dishes. "It's cold outside."

"He likes the fresh air," Sam answered without looking up.

He was carefully laying the five pieces of silver, polishing each article as he set it down. Next, he briskly rubbed the water glass, holding it up to the light to be sure no tiny blemish remained.

"Anybody'd think you're going to serve a banquet!

Minnie stood beside the screen. She was slightly annoyed. "You know those dishes are perfectly clean."

Sam looked at her. 'Did anybody ask you anything, Miss Minnie?" he inquired politely. "*I'm* setting this table."

"Well, I think—"

"That's the trouble," Sam interrupted, "*You think!* Dr. Carver *knows.*"

It was a good retort, in Dr. Carver's own style! Smiling broadly Sam returned to his work.

For some time now, he had been Dr. Carver's personal waiter. First, at his private table in the dining hall and now here. He was proud of that fact and had his own ideals about the job. No one could tell him what to do for Dr. Carver!

Visitors and curious ones now thronged to Tuskegee, swarming over the campus and peering through the halls asking, "Where is this Dr. Carver?" "What does he look like?" "Is he as strange as they say?" "Is he all Negro?" "Where is he?" "I want to see Carver!"

He knew their thoughts and as he grew older their idle curiosity annoyed him more and more. He refused to be put on exhibition. He had never really conquered the shyness of the frail, delicate little boy bewildered in a strange and alien world. He had his work to do.

They would have been shocked had they seen him eating behind the screen in a kitchen. But there, surrounded only by "other student workers," Dr. Carver found the privacy he wanted. There, during the rare moments of relaxation, he laughed and joked. Often, after the evening meal, when the last dish was washed and put away, they would linger around the kitchen table and he would talk. Here he'd say the things he never said on platforms or on radios. He knew the many obstacles in the long, hard road of these black boys and girls. Now, when he knew that he was approaching the end of the road, he chose this way to give them of his strength and wisdom and daily point out lessons they were never to forget.

"It's difficult for me to talk about Dr. Carver."

It was Sam Qualls speaking, many years later. Sam, now referred to as Samuel S. Qualls, Jr., head of his own successful business in Memphis, Tennessee, turned away. His eyes were fastened on a picture, framed and hung under special lighting in the wainscoted, dignified, high-ceilinged room.

Then he continued slowly, "We who were closest to Dr. Carver would like to shout his praises to the world. But—you see," he turned and his eyes were very deep and dark, "he wasn't that kind of a man. Sing about him, if you can, but don't shout!"

That November morning, back in the kitchen of Dorothy Hall, Minnie was not thinking of singing. She simply couldn't let Sam have the last word and as she picked up her tray to carry it into the dining room, she called out,

"Maybe you think you'll get a tip!"

She had gone before Sam could answer. And at that moment, Miss Sims, emerging from the pantry, asked with worry in her voice,

"Sam, do you suppose you'd have time to run over to the egg house before he comes? Three new people came in late last night and I'm afraid we're not going to have enough."

"No, ma'am, I'm sure I wouldn't." Sam was very positive.

"He's coming now." One of the waitresses had paused at the window.

"I haven't heard the bell." Miss Sims crossed the room quickly.

"Bell must be late." Sam filled his glass with water.

The outside door opened, admitting Dr. Carver. The collar of his coat was turned up and it was buttoned against the cold. The ragged, old cap was pulled down to his ears. In one hand he carried a large bunch of fern, the earth still clinging to the roots. Sam relieved him of the plants, noticing as he did so how cold and dry his hands were.

Then, with a courtly gesture the cap was whipped off and, "Good morning, young ladies." Dr. Carver bowed.

"Good morning, Dr. Carver."

The girls answered almost in unison. He hung his cap on a hook near the table. Turning down the coat collar and rubbing his hands together, he turned to Sam.

"And how's my loose-jointed young friend? Careful with those ferns. They're the last of the species I'll find this fall."

He watched while Sam placed the ferns in a pan and set them on a shelf. Then, together, they turned to the table. Sam pulled out Dr. Carver's chair and set a dish of sliced oranges before him.

"Did you see last night's paper?" Without pausing for a reply, he commented, "This coffee's very good—very good, indeed."

As if waiting for this observation Miss Sims appeared around the side of the screen.

"It's some of that which was sent you from Brazil. They'll be wanting to know how you liked it!"

And Miss Sims wrote something in her little notebook.

"It's fine." Dr. Carver's eyes twinkled. "Almost as good as my peanut coffee."

"What was in the paper last night?" Sam wanted to know.

"Paper? What paper?" Dr. Carver had forgotten.

"You asked me if I'd read last night's paper," Sam explained.

"Oh! Well, young man, do you read the evening paper?"

"Er—er—sometimes, but I didn't see—"

"In other words, you do *not* read the evening paper." His voice was severe. "Tck, tck! I don't know what I'm going to do with you!"

And he clicked his tongue disparagingly. He sighed deeply.

"Well, here it is." He pulled a newspaper from his pocket and then said quickly, "Now, don't bother me!"

Mystified, Sam unfolded the sheet. He knew there was something behind Dr. Carver's raillery, but—what? He turned a page. And then he saw. There in the center of the page was a picture of Dr. Carver. He was sort of "dressed up" and sat looking out from the sheet. Above the picture black letters announced, "Arthur Leroy Bainsfather's portrait of Carver takes the Blanche S. Benjamin prize of two hundred and fifty dollars for the loveliest painting of a Southern subject." He read further and learned that the prize had been awarded by the Southern States Art League at Montgomery, Alabama.

He looked up quickly and found Dr. Carver watching him, his bright eyes slightly veiled like a shy little boy.

"Oh! This is wonderful!" Sam rejoiced. He called out to the others.

"Give me back my paper!" Dr. Carver wanted to hide it, but they pulled it from his hands—read, looked, admired and exclaimed.

He really didn't mind, as long as it was just his "kitchen gang." A smile played about his lips. He remembered how he hadn't wanted to take time out to sit for that picture. He'd really been fidgety about the whole thing. He marveled himself at the "saintliness" of his expression when he recalled how anxious he had been to get away. It had seemed such a waste of time. He was glad now that the artist had won the prize. That was a little extraordinary. The reason given was: Spiritual rather than physical loveliness.

"Can you imagine that?" He chuckled. "Me—winning a beauty prize!"

Sam looked at him. Something in the boy's face must have touched the old man's heart. They smiled at each other and Sam said softly,

"Yes, sir. Yes, sir, I can imagine it!"

"You—you—lummox!" But his eyes shone brightly.

The outside world would not let him alone. The International Federation of Architects, Engineers, Chemists and Technicians chose Carver as the man of the year (1940) who had contributed most to science. Again heavy white cards were sent out in his honor and in the great dining hall of the Pennsylvania Hotel, New York City, the distinguished scholar, late Dr. Franz Boas, presented the stooped dark man with a bronze plaque for "distinguished service to humanity." Carver had come, ignoring advice of physicians, and now his response went ringing out over the air. Men were moved by his sincerity. They stirred at his insight and they laughed in delight at his keen wit.

A moving picture company brought its cameras, film and extras to Tuskegee to record the story of his life. Although this was a tremendous strain on his failing strength, he co-operated in every way. Perhaps some other poor boy would be encouraged.

Betsy Graves Reyneau came to paint him, but she did not ask that he "sit" for the picture.

"I wanted to catch him at his work, wearing the big, white apron made from flour sacks, his old shoes caked with mud, his hands tenderly touching the flowers he loved so much. I felt he should be out in the sunlight. So I painted him with his amaryllis—a flower with which he'd been working for years. See! At the bottom is the white amaryllis—his own creation, or, as he would have said, 'God's revelation' to him. His bare head and close-cropped white hair gave me a chance to do the marvelous skull with its tremendous development of frontal bones. He had the most aristocratic nose I've ever seen—high bridge and flaring nostrils. His whole face expresses overwhelming curiosity, soaring imagination and yet that shrewd and questioning doubt which bespeaks the true scientist."

"Ordinarily," she went on, "I should not have dared develop flowers in a portrait as I have done here. They would have distracted from the central figure. But his magnificent dark hands were powerful enough to compel attention and nothing could have taken from his face."

Now Sam Qualls had been graduated from Tuskegee and had returned to Memphis to work with his father.

"This wasn't what I had thought to do," he says, "I'd planned to go away and make a 'big name' for myself somewhere else. But I really hadn't the slightest idea what I wanted to do. Dr. Carver showed me that my job was right here. He told me I should do more and go further than my father had gone.

"I wrote him frequently and every Christmas I'd go back to see him. That last Christmas he was terribly anxious to know where all the other boys were."

"Ralph Stewart? Where is he now?"

"He's in the army—I think at Fort Huachuca."

Dr. Carver looked out the window a moment. He was growing feeble, but he chuckled with laughter.

"You remember the time I caught you two down in the basement roasting my peanuts?"

"Do I remember! What a tongue lashing you gave us!" Sam shivered as he recalled it.

Dr. Carver peered at him closely.

"Did you enjoy the peanuts?" he asked.

Sam nodded his head.

"They were worth all the trouble—those huge three-inch goobers!"

Dr. Carver shook his finger playfully.

"Still trying to flatter the old man, aren't you—lummox!"

Carver showed Sam the electric elevator Henry Ford had installed for him in Dorothy Hall, so that he wouldn't have to climb the nineteen steps from the laboratory entrance to his suite. "Exquisite elevator," he called it, as pleased as any child with a new toy.

He lived now in Dorothy Hall and took his meals in his own room. Everything was done to save him, but except on rare occasions he rose each morning and went to his laboratory.

Almost overnight Tuskegee campus had been transformed. Brown boys in smart, brown uniforms now walked proudly. Soon on their breasts appeared the widespread wings of the United States Air Corps, for just a few miles away was the Tuskegee Air Training School, an Air Base where young Negroes learned to fly.

In a world at war "Peace and good will" seemed to be bombed out of the skies and hearts of men. Where could they turn for hope and inspiration? Then, in November, 1942, a bill was introduced in Congress—a bill asking that a crumbling, old log cabin on a deserted farm in Missouri be transformed into a national shrine!

The *New York Herald Tribune* said, "We believe that Congress should act so that this memorial to an humble man whose achievements in a new land have been so great may be a present reaffirmation of the American principle of freedom of opportunity to all men alike."

There was no gaiety in Dorothy Hall on New Year's Day. Dr. Carver lay in a darkened room on the second floor.

Two weeks before on a cold, December morning, he had risen while it was still dark and, as was his custom, started out for the day's work. As he stepped off the side porch, he had slipped on the ice and fallen. Mrs. McAlister, the matron, heard his cry and hurried out to him. Two boys passing on the campus rushed across and as they helped him to his feet all urged:

"Don't go. We'll take you upstairs. You must lie down a little while."

He had said stubbornly, "I have work to do."

Leaning on the boys he had gone on to his laboratory where he said he'd be "all right." They left him then. Sometime afterwards he had gone to the office, limping a little, but had dictated letters, checked certain matters, talked at length with Austin Curtis. At noon, he returned to his room. He had not left it again.

There, propped up with pillows in bed, he painted charming Christmas cards which said "Peace on Earth and Good Will to Men."

18. A SHIP GOES OUT TO SEA

RAIN FELL IN ALABAMA. Her sun was shrouded in thick clouds of gray, her tears came softly down and soaked into the clays he had transformed, were cupped within the hearts of green things he had planted. Her best loved son lay dead.

Since early morning the long procession wound and curled far back of Dorothy Hall. Across the country they had come. In heavy wagons, trucks, in broken, old cars, many on foot—they had come over bad roads, through woods and swamps, the people he had served, who loved him. Old men and young, women and girls, white and black, school children, carrying their books and lunches, cripples who only a year ago could not have walked at all—the mist still fell on them as they stood patiently waiting their turn to see his face.

He lay within a lovely bower of flowers—flowers in huge frames and stacked in heaps about him. They hovered over him with tender watchfulness, and shed their radiance with a joyful pride. Light from the stained-glass windows filtered down and fell upon his face—fine cut and chiseled ebony against the creamy satin. He wore his best suit, with the usual white flower stuck in lapel.

All the facilities of the small town and Institute had been taxed to the utmost. Telegrams and messages poured in. From the Carver clan in Missouri came this word, "We should be honored to receive the body of George Washington Carver and inter it in the family lot at Diamond Grove. Here are the mountains that he loved. The Ozark mountains claim him as their own."

As the hour approached, soldiers marched upon the campus and officers in full dress uniform stood at attention. Blue-coated army cadets threw open the doors of the chapel and they marched in. Cameras clicked and notables from far and near humbly slipped into their places. Last came his co-workers, wearing no sign of mourning—only the jaunty white flower in their lapels. They knew he would like this.

It was a simple service. Words were not needed. Music by fresh, young voices of the Tuskegee Choir, singing the songs he had loved best. Among the messages read were those from the President of the United States, from the Vice-President, that little boy whom he had led to "see more than I knew was there" and from Chief Justice Black. Then the quiet words of the Chaplain:

And so they gave a ship his name . . .

"For God so loves the world
He gives His most beloved
sons that men shall live . . ."

None of the many products of his brain and hands can be used to destroy—not one!

And so they gave a ship his name—The Liberty Ship, *George Washington Carver*. All the people cheered as, proudly, it slipped into the mighty Pacific Ocean, quivering a little as the white spray rose to the blue dome of sky. Then, it was poised lightly as the body settled.

They watched it go to sea, those throngs gathered on the bank. They joined hands, singing a new song—*It is made manifest*. Words became timber and steel and strength—*hope and peace and good-will to all men*. What is in a name? Wherever the good ship, *George Washington Carver*, goes, men will know the human spirit cannot be suppressed nor dignity of service be denied. They will have before their eyes the evidence that the dauntless spirit of a great American lives on.

DR. GEORGE WASHINGTON CARVER'S LIFE IN BRIEF

Born: Diamond Grove, Missouri, of slave parents, 1864.
Received High School Training: Minneapolis, Kansas.
Attended Simpson College: Indianola, Iowa.
Received Degree of B.S. from Iowa State College of Agriculture
    at Ames, Iowa, in 1894.
Received Degree of M.S. in Agriculture from Iowa State College
    in 1896. Appointed member of Faculty of Iowa State College.
Accepted position at Tuskegee, 1896.
First Director of Agriculture at Tuskegee Institute.
Appointed Director of Research and Experiment Station which
    was established by an Act of the State Legislature in 1896.
Elected Fellow, Royal Society of Arts, London, England, 1916.
Appeared before Congressional Ways and Means Committee,
    1921.
Awarded Spingarn Medal, 1923.
Doctor of Science Degree was conferred by Simpson College,
    Indianola, Iowa, 1928.
Appointed Collaborator, Mycology and Plant Disease Survey,
    Bureau of Plant Industry, United States Department of Agri-
    culture, 1935.
Awarded Roosevelt Medal for distinguished service in Science,
    1939.
Awarded Plaque for distinguished service by International Fed-
    eration of Architects, Engineers, Chemists, and Technicians,
    1940.
Received Certificate of Award and was made a member of The
    League of the Golden Hearts, February 17, 1941, by Presby-
    terian Church of Vernon, Texas.
Awarded citation for distinguished service to humanity by Cath-

olic Conference of the South, Birmingham, Alabama, April 22, 1941.

Received Humanitarian Award of Plaque and $1,000.00 from The Variety Clubs of America at Atlantic City, New Jersey, May 17, 1941.

Degree of Doctor of Science conferred by University of Rochester, June 18, 1941.

Died at Tuskegee Institute, January 5, 1943.

A few of the leading Universities and Colleges where Dr. Carver spoke:

Duke University, New York University, Yale University, Furman University, University of North Carolina, Greensboro College for Women, Howard University, Washington College, Mississippi State College for Women.

Dr. Carver developed from peanuts, wild plums, sweet potatoes, cotton, cowpeas, and from indigenous plants many useful products.

Dr. Carver advocated ways of developing Southern resources, and published numerous bulletins.

CARVER MUSEUM

The Trustees of Tuskegee Institute in April, 1938, voted the brick building adjacent to Dorothy Hall on the main campus highway to become the Carver Museum to house Dr. Carver's priceless collections, his offices and laboratories, and the office of Dr. Carver's assistant.

The Carver Museum, through a wide variety of exhibits, gives some idea of the versatility and industry of Dr. Carver. Here may be seen paints, stains and varnishes from Alabama clay, artificial marble made from wood shavings, beautiful wall hangings from feed sacks and wrapping strings, rugs and mats from okra and iron weed fiber, charming landscapes from water colors that started off as coffee grounds and osage orange peels. Here the farmer may study diseases of common crops in various stages of development.

In the Museum are Alabama fruits and vegetables canned 35 years ago to encourage farmers to grow vegetables and to show farm wives how to cook, dry and preserve them—the fore-runner of the present farm and home demonstration work of the Extension Service of the U. S. Department of Agriculture. Here may be seen also plastics, ceramics, as well as more than 300 products from the peanut, 118 from the sweet potato, and hun-dreds from waste materials.

On November 17, 1941, the rooms housing the Carver Art Collection were opened to the public. Here the visitor may see Dr. Carver's paintings in oil, and paints made from Alabama clays. One of his paintings, The Three Peaches, done with his fingers and with the pigments he has developed from the clays of Ala-bama—has been requested by the famous Luxemburg Gallery in Europe. One room houses his collection of needlework containing hundreds of patterns made by Dr. Carver in his spare moments.

RESULTS OF HIS CREATIVE RESEARCH

Dr. Carver developed:

From clays of Alabama—face powder, pigments, paints, stains.

From Peanuts—over 300 products: milk, cream, buttermilk, cheese, condiments, coffee, plastics, paper, stains, insuiating boards, flour, etc.

From Sweet Potatoes—118 products: starch, tapioca, mock cocoanut, syrup, breakfast food, stains, flour, etc.

From Cotton—Paving blocks, insulating boards, cordage, paper and rugs.

From waste materials—Numerous useful products.

II

THE GEORGE WASHINGTON CARVER FOUNDATION

On February 10, 1940, the George Washington Carver Foundation was incorporated under the laws of the State of Alabama and from that date possessed:

A. The power and right to receive property of any nature, kind or character, by gift, will or devise, holding the same in conformity with all lawful conditions imposed by the Donor.

B. The right to acquire and hold real and personal property, or any other kind of property or things of use and value, in the carrying out of the plan and purposes of this Foundation.

The Objectives of the Foundation are:

1. To expand and perpetuate the research work of Dr. George W. Carver, a pioneer of Farm Chemurgy.
2. To complete many of the research projects under investigation by Dr. Carver, which are at the present time most favorable and promising as to results.
3. To coordinate and correlate research from the soil to the complete product.
4. To develop products from farm crops, waste products and native vegetation.
5. To attempt to develop new varieties of plants for specific industrial purposes.
6. To study influence of soil types and fertilizing practices on chemical composition of plants.
7. To demonstrate the industrial application of processes developed and products produced.

(Tuskegee Bulletin on Foundation, 1940)

III

THE GEORGE WASHINGTON CARVER
NATIONAL MONUMENT

Richard Pilant has been the leader in the movement to establish the birthplace of Dr. Carver as a national monument. In April, 1942, by order of Governor Forest Donnell, an official marker was erected on Federal Highway 71, designating the birthplace. January 7, 1943, the Missouri House of Representatives paused to mark Dr. Carver's death and pay tribute to his memory and on January 28, Missouri House and Senate unanimously passed a resolution urging that Congress adopt the bill which was to come up for hearing before the Public Lands Committee, February 5.

Mr. Pilant was born at Grandby, Mo., six miles from the birthplace of George Washington Carver. He was blind until he was ten years old.

"Perhaps," he says, "that's why I can understand so well what Dr. Carver meant when he says people do not 'see.'"

"I was early aware of Dr. Carver as 'the greatest man our district has produced.' That's what they told all the children white and colored, in our schools."

Mr. Pilant appeared before this Committee as the representative of the people of Missouri. He came with thousands of signatures.

"We Missourians are determined that the world shall never forget that it was from our Ozark hills Dr. Carver took his origin. We cannot but believe that it was to these faraway hills of his childhood that Dr. Carver looked when he said, as he was wont to do, 'look to the hills from whence cometh comfort, lift up thine eyes to the Hills!' One born in these hills may become by turns a Kansan, an Iowan, an Alabaman, but he never ceases to be a Missourian. One cannot become a native of these hills by adoption, only by birth, and it is to the place of his birth rather than the color of a man's skin or the fatness of his pocketbook that we look. Like that other great Missourian, Mark Twain, we have no regard for pomp and parade, show and sham—nothing but the essential man matters, and that is all that matters."

(Signed) Richard Pilant,
Washington University, St. Louis, Missouri, March 1, 1943.

78TH *CONGRESS*—1ST SESSION
H. R. 647

IN THE HOUSE OF REPRESENTATIVES

JANUARY 6, 1943

Mr. SHORT introduced the following bill; which was referred to
the Committee on the Public Lands

A BILL

To provide for the establishment of the George Washington
Carver National Monument.

1   *Be it enacted by the Senate and House of Representa-*
2   *tives of the United States of America in Congress assembled,*
3   That the Secretary of the Interior is authorized and directed
4   to acquire, on behalf of the United States, by gift or purchase,
5   the site of the birthplace of George Washington Carver,
6   distinguished Negro scientist, located near Diamond, Missouri,
7   together with such additional land and any improvements
8   thereon as the Secretary may deem necessary to carry out the
9   purposes of this Act. In the event the Secretary is unable
10   to acquire such property, or any part thereof, at a reasonable
11   price, he is authorized and directed to condemn such prop-
12   erty, or any part thereof, in the manner provided by law.
13   SEC. 2. The property acquired under the provisions of
14   section 1 of this Act shall constitute the George Washington
15   Carver National Monument and shall be a public national
16   memorial to George Washington Carver. The Director of
17   the National Park Service, under the direction of the Secre-
18   tary of the Interior, shall have the supervision, management,
19   and control of such national monument, and shall maintain
20   and preserve it for the benefit and enjoyment of the people
21   of the United States.
22   SEC. 3. The Secretary of the Interior is authorized to—
23   (1) Maintain, either in an existing structure acquired
24   under the provisions of section 1 of this Act or in a build-
25   ing constructed by him for the purpose, a museum for relics
26   and records pertaining to George Washington Carver, and

27 for other articles of national and patriotic interest, and to
28 accept, on behalf of the United States, for installation in
29 such museum, articles which may be offered as additions
30 to the museum; and
31   (2) Construct roads and mark with monuments, tablets,
32 or otherwise, points of interest within the boundaries of the
33 George Washington Carver National Monument.
34   SEC. 4. There are authorized to be appropriated such
35 sums as may be necessary to carry out the provisions of this
36 Act.

IV

THE CARVER ART COLLECTION

Now in the Carver Museum at Tuskegee Institute,
Tuskegee, Alabama.

GROUP I

This group consists of twenty-seven oil paintings on canvas,
done at Simpson College, School of Art, Indianola, Iowa, under
the direction of Miss Etta M. Budd nearly or quite fifty years
ago. Most of them are landscapes done in pastel shades. As ex-
amples:

No. 3. A Quiet Little Brook: dainty and expressive.

    4. Yucca, Angustifolia and Cactus: Two plants indige-
       nous to the dry arid plains of Western Kansas.
          This is the painting done from memory nearly fif-
          teen years after the plant was seen. It was given
          honorable mention at the World's Columbian Ex-
          position in May, 1893.

    6. Evening Twilight:
          Consists of a soft, dreamy, bit of landscape.

  11. The Village Church:
          Suggests quietness, rest and worship.

  17. Dutch Wharf:
          Another of the four selected for the World's Co-
          lumbian Exposition.

  25. Some Rare Orchids:
          Very much at home on an old fence post.

Nine paintings done with Alabama clays:

No. 1. A still life study consisting of a cantaloupe, bunch of grapes, against a mystic background.
3. Some rare pond lilies.
5. Landscape showing foundation work.
8. Four Peaches.
This is an exquisite study.
9. A water color study in blue and white.

MISCELLANEOUS GROUP

The pictures in this group are many and varied, consisting of oil, charcoal, water color, china, pen and pencil sketches, Christmas cards, pastels and quite a number of a very unique group of small water color studies done in the Curtis Browns.

V

BULLETINS PREPARED BY DR. CARVER

The bulletins listed below are available for general distribution. A limited budget and the expense connected with the publishing of these bulletins limits free distribution to farm families.

BULLETINS

No. 24. The Pickling and Curing of Meat in Hot Weather—Price 20¢

No. 31. How to Grow the Peanut and 105 Ways to Prepare it for Human Consumption—Price 25¢

No. 36. How to Grow the Tomato and 115 Ways to Prepare it for the Table—Price 25¢

No. 38. How the Farmer Can Save His Sweet Potatoes—Price 20¢

No. 40. The Raising of Hogs—Price 10¢

No. 41. Can Livestock be Raised Profitably in Alabama—Price 15¢

No. 42. How to Build Up and Maintain the Virgin Fertility of our Soils—Price 15¢

No. 43. Nature's Garden for Victory and Peace—Price 20¢
Agricultural Research and Experiment Station,
Tuskegee Institute, Alabama.
A. W. CURTIS, JR., *Director*.

A BULLETIN
"NATURE'S GARDEN FOR VICTORY AND PEACE"
February 14, 1942
By GEORGE W. CARVER

DANDELION (Taraxacum officinale). This is the ordinary dandelion of our dooryard, field and road sides, with which we are more or less familiar. It is very tender and delicious now (February 20) and may be served in a variety of appetizing ways. (Use leaves only.)
1. Wash, prepare, and cook exactly the same as turnip or collard greens.
2. Prepare the same as spinach with hard boiled eggs.
3. A simple, plain and appetizing salad may be made thus:
    1 pint of finely shredded young dandelion leaves
    1 medium sized onion, finely chopped
    2 small radishes, finely chopped
    1 tablespoon of minced parsley
    1 tablespoon of sugar (can be left out)
       Salt and pepper to taste.

Moisten thoroughly with weak vinegar or mayonnaise, mix, place in salad dish and garnish with slices of hard boiled egg and pickled beets. This is only one of the many delicious and appetizing salads that will readily suggest themselves to the resourceful housewife.

Aside from the dandelion's value for food, it is well known and highly prized for its many curative properties.

CURLED DOCK (Rumex Crispus). This is often called our native rhubarb; grows in abundance almost everywhere and is one of the very best of our wild greens; relished almost universally. Cook the same as turnip greens. Many like it prepared the same as spinach. The root of this plant is highly prized as a blood medicine.

PEPPER-GRASS (Lepidium species). There are several varieties of this common dooryard and garden plant. It belongs to the mustard family and can be cooked in the same way. It is delicious when prepared as an uncooked salad, the same as recommended for dandelion.

WATER GRASS (Nasturtium officinale). This plant is too well known to need description here. As a pot herb, garnishing salads, etc., it has few equals. There are many different types growing in both swamps and upland.

THE WEED'S PHILOSOPHY

As presented by Dr. Carver in his bulletin "Nature's Garden for Victory and Peace."

Nay, but tell me, am I not unlucky indeed,
To arise from the earth and be only a weed?
Ever since I came out of my dark little seed,
I have tried to live rightly, but still am a—weed!

To be torn by the roots and destroyed, this my meed,
And despised by the gardener, for being a weed.
Ah! but why was I born, when man longs to be freed
Of a thing so obnoxious and bad as a weed?

Now, the cause of myself and my brothers I plead,
Say, can any good come of my being a weed?
If a purpose divine is in all things decreed,
Then there must be some benefit from me, a—weed!

If of evil and suffering, the world still has need
In its path of development, then I, a weed,
Must form part of that plan which in nature I read,
Though I live but to die, just for being a weed!

—MARTHA MARTIN.

MISCELLANEOUS DISHES FROM PEANUTS
From Bulletin No. 31
Experiment Station, Tuskegee Institute, Alabama
By GEORGE W. CARVER

No. 10—English Peanut Bread.
  2 cups liquid yeast,
  1 tablespoon butter,
  2 tablespoons sugar,
  1 teaspoon of salt,
  1 cup finely-chopped blanched peanuts.

Flour as long as you can stir it with a spoon; beat it long and hard; let stand in a warm place until light; add peanuts, add flour to make a soft dough; beat well, let stand in a warm place until it rises again; bake in a moderate oven one hour.

No. 36—Peanut Strips with Bananas.
  2 cups mashed banana pulp,
  1 cup wheat flakes,
  1 cup flour,
  1 cup peanut meal,
  1 cup sugar,
  ½ cup creamed butter,
  1 saltspoon of salt.

Blend all together; roll out one-half of an inch thick, cut in strips and bake in quick oven.

No. 39—Mock Veal Cutlets.

Wash one cup of lentils, soak over night; in the morning strain and parboil in fresh boiling water for 30 minutes; drain again, and cook until soft in sufficient water to cover them; rub through a sieve, to the puree add ¼ cup of melted butter, 1 cup of fine Graham bread crumbs, 1 cup of strained tomatoes to which a speck of soda has been added, 1 cup chopped peanuts, 1 tablespoon each of grated celery and minced onion; season with ¼ teaspoon mixed herbs, salt and pepper; blend all thoroughly together and form into cutlets; dip in egg and then dip in fine bread crumbs; place in a well-greased baking pan, and brown in quick oven; arrange around a mound of well-seasoned mashed potatoes, serve with brown sauce.

No. 38—Mock Chicken.

Blanch and grind one cup of peanuts until they are quite oily; stir in one well-beaten egg; thicken with rolled bread crumbs; stir in little salt. Boil some sweet potatoes until done, peel and cut in thin slices, spread generously with peanut mixture; dip in white of egg; fry to a chicken brown; serve hot.

No. 43—Peanut and Cheese Roast.

> 1 cup grated cheese,
> 1 cup finely-ground peanuts,
> 1 cup bread crumbs,
> 1 teaspoon chopped onion,
> 1 tablespoon butter,
> Juice of half a lemon,
> Salt and pepper to taste.

Cook the onion in the butter and a little water until it is tender. Mix the other ingredients, and moisten with water, using the water in which the onion has been cooked. Pour into a shallow baking dish, and brown in the oven.

No. 81—Peanut Divinity Fudge.

> 2½ cups sugar,
> ½ cup syrup,
> ½ cup water,
> 2 eggs,
> 1 cup coarsely-broken peanuts.

Boil the sugar, syrup, and water together until, when dropped in cold water, the mixture will form a hard ball between the fingers; beat the eggs stiff; pour half the boiling mixture over eggs, beating constantly; return remaining half of the mixture to the stove, and boil until it forms a hard ball when dropped into cold water; remove from the stove, and pour slowly into first half, beating constantly; add peanuts, and flavor with vanilla; pour into a buttered pan, and cut in squares.

No. 91—Peanut Almond Fudge (very fine).

    1 cup peanuts deeply browned. **Crush or grind.**
1½ cups sugar,
    1 cup milk,
    1 tablespoon butter,
    1 teaspoon almond extract.

Brown ½ cup of sugar in a granite pan; add the milk; when the brown sugar is thoroughly dissolved add one cup of granulated sugar and the butter; boil to the soft-ball stage; flavor with extract; add peanuts; beat until creamy; pour into buttered tins, and mark off into squares.

SOME SIMPLE METHODS OF DRYING FRUITS AND VEGETABLES

From Bulletin No. 43, Experiment Station, Tuskegee Institute
By GEORGE W. CARVER

FRUITS

Begin drying just as soon as the seed matures, or as soon as the fruit is two-thirds ripe, and continue as long as you can handle it without mashing to a pulp.

Caution—In drying either fruits or vegetables in the sun, screen wire or mosquito netting should be stretched over a suitable frame to keep off flies and other insects; and everything must be scrupulously clean.

PLUMS—NO. 1

Select medium ripe plums, cover with boiling water, cover the vessel and let stand twenty minutes; drain and spread in the sun to dry. Stir occasionally; when dry examine them frequently and at the first appearance of worms put in the oven and heat for a few minutes. In cooking, soak in cold water for a few hours the same as for other dried fruit.

PLUMS—NO. 2

After peeling plums, allow half pound of sugar to one pound of fruit. Put fruit and sugar in layers in a preserving kettle. Heat slowly until sugar is dissolved, then boil until clear. Spread the fruit on platters in the sun and turn over until quite dry. Pack in layers with sugar in stone jars.

GRAPES

Gather when ripe, wash, put in porcelain or granite preserving kettle, cover with boiling water, let simmer until the berries are hot through and the hulls have turned a reddish color, now stir in a scant tablespoon of baking soda to the gallon of fruit, stir well for three minutes, but do not mash the fruit; drain off this water, wash in three more waters, being careful each time not to mash the berries. They may now be dried whole or made into a leather.

VEGETABLES

CORN

Corn is delicious when dried. Take tender roasting ears; steam until nearly done; cut from the cob with a sharp knife; spread thinly upon boards; put in the sun to dry. If the top of the grains are shaved off and the pulp scraped out, leaving most of the husk on the cob, it makes a finer product. In cooking, it should be soaked for an hour or two in cold water before the final cooking.

STRING BEANS

Select very young tender beans, wash and cut off both the stem and blossom ends. Cut into one-inch lengths, steam until about one-fourth done or until they lose their grass green appearance. Spread on trays and dry as any other fruit or vegetable. Soak for several hours in cold water before cooking.

VI

BIBLIOGRAPHY

"Pioneers of Plenty—the Story of Chemurgy," by Christy Borth. Enlarged Edition, The Bobbs-Merrill Company, New York City, 1942.

"The Man Who Talks with the Flowers," by Glenn Clark. Macalester Park Publishing Co., St. Paul, Minnesota, 1938.

"The Movable School Goes to the Negro Farmer," by Thomas Monroe Campbell. Tuskegee Institute Press, Tuskegee Institute, Alabama, 1926.

"Contemporary Immortals," by Archibald Henderson. D. Appleton Co., London & New York, 1930.

"Portraits in Color," by Mary White Ovington. The Viking Press, New York City, 1927.

"A Boy Who Was Traded for a Horse," by James Saxon Childers. *American Magazine*, October, 1932.

"Forty Years of Creative Research Work," by Austin W. Curtis, Jr. *The Peanut Journal and Nut World*, Suffolk, Virginia, March, 1937.

"The Wizard of Tuskegee," by W. Wade Moss. *The Chemist*, October, 1936, publication of American Institute of Chemists, Inc., New York City.

Congressional Record, January, 1921—Hearings of Ways and Means Committee.

Book of Newspaper Clippings on George W. Carver in the Shomberg Collection, New York Public Library.

VII

ACKNOWLEDGMENT

FOR THE GENEROUS ASSISTANCE OF

Austin W. Curtis, Director, George Washington Carver Foundation.

Thomas M. Campbell, U. S. Field Agent, Department of Agriculture.

Myrle Cooper, Superintendent Tuskegee Green Houses.

Henry C. Baker, oldest farmer in Macon County, Alabama.

Mrs. Beatrice B. Walcott, Red Cross Director, Tuskegee, Alabama.

Sanford E. Lee, County Agricultural Agent, State of Georgia.

Samuel W. Qualls, Qualls & Son Funeral Home, Memphis, Tenn.

Richard Pilant, Washington University, St. Louis, Mo.

Helen Ferris, Editor-in-Chief, Junior Literary Guild.

And to all those who, loving him, were glad to add some enlightening word,

WE THANK YOU

INDEX

Adams, Lewis, 125
Agricultural College of Iowa, 88
Agriculture, Department of, 10, 200
Ames, 109, 117, 129, 205
Armstrong, General, 125

Barnard, Harry, 159
Big Nat, 71-73, 96
Black, Chief Justice, 226
boll weevil, 153, 154, 160
Borth, Christy, 159
Brown, Dan, 105-108
Budd, Etta M., 108

Campbell, Thomas M., 133, 134, 151
Carew, Mr., 88
Carver Art Collection, 237, 238
Carver, Farmer Moses, and wife, 11-31, 33-43, 44-46, 50, 51, 53, 75-79, 99, 226
Carver, George Washington, first trip to Washington, 3-11; goes sightseeing, 6-11; finds dangerous fungi on plant, 10; recognized as mycologist, 9; speaks before Senate Committee, 11, 81-89; works on farm, 12, 13; his father is killed, 15; he and his mother are stolen, 16-18; is ransomed, 17-19; loses voice, 18, 19; cares for garden, 22-24; his brother leaves home, 21-24; he finds bugs on apple tree, 23, 24; the fish pond, 25, 26, 29, 30; makes a bird's nest, 26, 27; raises grapes, 33, 34; trip to Jaegars, 34-43; school-days, 44-61; home with the Martins, 48-57; home with Aunt Mariah Watkins, 57-61; school in

Kansas, 62-67, 70; runs a laundry, 62, 63; works on railroad, 67-70; cooks at ranch, 67; picks fruit in New Mexico, 70; barber's helper, 71-73, 75; home with the Seymours, 73-76; his brother dies, 75; visits the Carvers, 76-79; testifies on uses of peanuts, 83-89; refused admission at Highland University, 91-93; a "homesteader," 96, 97; makes friends with the Millhollands, 100-107; studies music, 104, 105; attends Simpson College, 106-109; studies art, 108; attends Iowa State College, 109-121; lives in James Wilson's office, 110; military training, 112-116; is commissioned Lieutenant, 116; meets Henry Wallace, 117-120; official "rubber" for athletes, 120; received his B.S. from Iowa State, 121; commissioned Captain in U. S. Officers Reserve, 121; paintings exhibited at Columbian Exposition, 121; appointed teacher of botany at Iowa State, 122, 123, 126, 127; offered work at Tuskegee, 127, 128; received M.S. degree at Iowa State University, 130; builds and equips laboratory out of scrap, 136, 137; uses first two-horse plow, 137; makes paint from clay, 141-143; gives concert tour for Tuskegee, 147, 148; sets up program to aid his race, 149, 150; plants peanuts in place of cotton, 153-156; uses of peanuts, 154-159; made member of Royal Society for the Encour-

About the Authors

SHIRLEY GRAHAM was born in Indiana, the daughter of a Methodist minister, and raised in parsonages all over the country. In high school she was elected class poet and her essay on Booker T. Washington took first place for literary distinction. She has studied at the Sorbonne in Paris and at Oberlin College in Ohio where she took her Master's Degree. In 1938 she was awarded a Julius Rosenwald Fellowship for Creative Writing, and in 1947 she received a Guggenheim Fellowship. Miss Graham travels around the world a great deal, but she makes Brooklyn, New York, her home.

GEORGE D. LIPSCOMB attended high school in Freeport, Illinois, where he won a state oratorical contest which carried a scholarship to Northwestern University. He won various oratorical awards at college and the Sargent Prize in literary interpretation. After leaving Northwestern, he taught for thirteen years in the Negro colleges of the South as Professor of English and Speech Arts. He is the author of several plays, textbooks on speech and a number of stories for young people.